NEAR-DEATH EXPERIENCES:

True stories of Near-Death Experiences:

True Stories of going to Heaven

Rachel J. Hopkins

Copyright 2023

Near-Death Experiences

Table of Contents

Introduction 6

Chapter One: Daniel Ardita 8

Chapter Two: Cyril 13

Chapter Three: Dr. Pertierra 16

Chapter Four: Claudius 19

Chapter Five: Oscar Berlanga 21

Chapter Six: Siri Karlsen 23

Chapter Seven: David Milarch 25

Chapter Eight: Kate Cliff 29

Chapter Nine: Christine Stein 31

Chapter Ten: Dr. Bellg 33

Chapter Eleven: Dennis Hale 35

Chapter Twelve: Titus Rivas 38

Chapter Thirteen: George de Benneville 40

Chapter Fourteen: Destiny 42

Chapter Fifteen: Ray Kilman 46

Near-Death Experiences

Chapter Sixteen: Dr. Turner 50

Chapter Seventeen: Kathy Baker 53

Chapter Eighteen: Peggy Abernethy 55

Chapter Nineteen: Bryan MIller 57

Chapter Twenty: Dave Faler 59

Chapter Twenty-One: Jane Smith 61

Chapter Twenty-Two: Charmain Edwards 64

Chapter Twenty-Three: Martha St Claire 67

Chapter Twenty-Four: Steve 71

Chapter Twenty-Five: Robert Leo 74

Chapter Twenty-Six: Jim Anderson 77

Chapter Twenty-Seven: Dr.Martin 79

Chapter Twenty-Eight: Emma Offers 82

Chapter Twenty-Nine: Barbara Whitefield 84

Chapter Thirty: Chris Markey 87

Chapter Thirty-One: Hamish Miller 89

Chapter Thirty-Two: Diane Sherman 92

Chapter Thirty-Three: Erica McKenzie 94

Chapter Thirty-Four: Jessica Haynes 96

Chapter Thirty-Five: Dr. Ebby 98

Near-Death Experiences

Chapter Thirty-Six: Priscilla McGill 102

Chapter Thirty-Seven: Daniel Ditchfield 104

Chapter Thirty-Eight: Andrea Von Wilomonsky 107

Chapter Thirty-Nine: Rune Fagerheim 109

Chapter Forty: Scott 116

Chapter Forty-One: Fraun Cristostomo 121

Chapter Forty-Two: Ruby Cassimo 122

Chapter Forty-Three: Mr. A 124

Chapter Forty-Four: Annabel Beam 126

Chapter Forty-Five: Jack 127

Chapter Forty-Six: Lynn 128

Chapter Forty-Seven: Dr. Pertierra 129

Chapter Forty-Eight: Michaela 131

Chapter Forty-Nine: Stephan Horenstein 132

Chapter Fifty: Arthur 134

Chapter Fifty-One: Tommy Laux 136

Chapter Fifty-Two: Maria 138

Chapter Fifty-Three: Vincent 139

Chapter Fifty-Four: Fabienne 141

Chapter Fifty-five: Stephanie 144

Near-Death Experiences

Chapter Fifty-Six: Nicole Canivenq 148

Chapter Fifty-Seven: Sylvie 151

Chapter Fifty-Eight: Valerie 153

Chapter Fifty-Nine: Sophie 155

Chapter Sixty: Natalie 156

Chapter Sixty-One: Mo Abdelbaki 158

Chapter Sixty-Two: Nadi McCaffrey 160

Chapter Sixty-Three: Philip 164

Chapter Sixty-Four: Maria 167

Chapter Sixty-Five: Dr. Greyson 169

Chapter Sixty-Six: Louis Tucker 171

Chapter Sixty-Seven: Cherie 173

Chapter Sixty-Eight: Joe Tiralosi 175

Chapter Sixty-Nine: Chamise 177

Chapter Seventy: Gillian 179

Conclusion 182

Near-Death Experiences

Introduction

This book contains some of the most remarkable, compelling, and comforting true stories of people who have had Near-Death Experiences. These people describe finding themselves in Heaven. Their stories are astonishing, and from these stories we are given a glimpse of what really happens to us when we die, of where we go, of what Heaven is really like, and how each and every person who got taken there, simply cannot wait to go back there again. They say it felt like home. It felt like where they truly belonged, and the overwhelming unconditional love they received there was like nothing they had ever known before; total pure all-encompassing love, joy and forgiveness.

Have you ever wanted to know what happens when a person has a Near-Death experience?

Have you ever wanted to know what happens when you die?

Have you ever wanted to know if Heaven really does exist?

Near-Death Experiences

The stories in this book will answer those questions....

Chapter One: Daniel Ardita

Daniel Ardita was born in Argentina. He now works in green architecture and permaculture, after his life forever was altered by his near-death experience in 2006. It happened when he was 35 years old and living in Madrid. He was working as a lawyer specialising in international law. He has told his extraordinary story to news outlets including inuovivespri.it. He says, "I was living a normal life where it was important to me to live well, make money and achieve my personal goals. Death for me was a state of matter; I didn't believe in the afterlife nor in any type of religion, even if I grew up according to the dogmas of the catholic religion. At the time of my accident, one of my passions was travelling by motorcycle, and I was at the pinnacle of my life, sailing with the wind at my back, having achieved professional success teaching at the University of Madrid and I was financially well-off and enjoying the freedom of being single – until suddenly life slapped me to wake me up. I was riding my motorbike on a small road, at 120 mph. I didn't realise a car was

Near-Death Experiences

coming round the bend. I tried to dodge it, but it was useless. I had no helmet, just a bathing suit. I was just going to the beach. The windshield of the car impacted my chest, breaking my sternum and three ribs. My head hit the roof of the car... and this is where the real journey begins. Suddenly, an impressive light appeared, everything was white; the ground, the sky, in front of me, everything was an intense white, and I felt indescribable peace, an indescribable tranquillity. In that instant, images of my life suddenly began to pass through me from when I was little up to the last moments. A succession of images and a background, similar to that of a cassette when playing fast forward. I couldn't understand a word, but an understanding came to me of what I believed it was to be alive. In that moment, it was like a dialogue, where I realised the most important things that I had always taken for granted. I thought, 'I'm dead. I'm dying,' and an anxiety seized me, and the first thing that came to mind were my children. I clearly felt a presence that had no body but that I could feel as if I was looking into his eyes." Then, it all stopped, and he found himself back again. "I went back, and instantly it was like falling with a parachute from the sky." Daniel says he brought back knowledge with him. "A voice taught me how to heal myself – the voice like a fast-paced cassette tape told me that humans have the power to speak to every cell in their body. At that moment, an image like a tube with a bubble in

Near-Death Experiences

the centre appeared. It told me I had to raise my heartbeat and my body temperature and visualise this bubble decreasing, and they showed me my ribs and that I had to visualise a golden white ray and see how the bones should be reconstructed. I didn't understand if it was really voices speaking to me or if I was going crazy from the blow to my head." In the hospital the following day, Daniel was taken for another CT scan and ultrasound. "I felt fine, I wanted to get out of the hospital, but three doctors came for me. They sat me down. The senior doctor told me, "Yesterday, you entered the hospital with a severe head trauma, and in the CT scan we saw a bubble – a clot that formed from the impact. In this morning's CT scan, the clot has disappeared. We can't believe it – it's a miracle. We call it a case of spontaneous recovery." One day later, Daniel was discharged from hospital. When he went to his GP a few days later, the GP said his x-ray results showed that his broken ribs had almost healed already. Daniel was dumfounded and perplexed. "I wanted answers – my highly sceptical structured thinking, accustomed to rational logic, was looking for evidence of the existence of the miracle. I wanted to understand with reason. "

"The surprise came during the week of my return from hospital. I was feeling good, and some friends invited me to a party where I met a girl. We ended up spending the night in her apartment. After making love, it was 5 a.m, the

Near-Death Experiences

whole house was dark, and I was suddenly woken up. There was a gentleman who was grabbing my toe and he was telling me he didn't want us to make love in his daughter's room. From the fright I took, I nudged the girl who was asleep and told her to turn on the light. As soon as she turned on the light, she asked me what was wrong. I had scared her. At that moment, I looked at her and thought that if I told her what I'd seen, she would think I was crazy. The first night I know her, and I tell her what I saw! No, I thought. But finally, I told her, and she actually told me that I wasn't crazy and that I'd seen the dead. "What was the ghost like?" she asked me. So, I told her what this gentleman looked like: an old man with white hair and a blue jacket with two front pockets. The girl began to change her expression – she was afraid. "Your describing my father!" This was the first of several paranormal experiences until I realized I needed to find someone to help me. When I met people, I would receive images that I did not understand. One day, I told my story to a friend, who after listening, suggested I visit a spiritual medium." When Daniel arrived at the medium's house, she knew nothing about Daniel, not even his name, but she told him, "You broke three ribs and your sternum." These were the injuries he had received in his motorbike crash. Daniel says, "She explained to me that there were faculties that had woken up during the accident." After Daniel's near-death experience, he gave up his lawyer's lifestyle and all that went with it. He

Near-Death Experiences

changed his life completely, living a simple, unmaterialistic life now with few needs. He says, "I am not afraid of death; death accompanies me every day. The most important thing is to be present here and now, without any expectations..."

Near-Death Experiences

Chapter Two: Cyril

41-year-old Cyril told his story to Alanna Fox, who runs a lifestyle blog called Alanna.lifeblog. Cyril had a near-death experience at the age of 11 when he went swimming with his school class. At the time, he was simply sitting at the edge of the pool, when one of his classmates decided to push him into the deep end. As Cyril sunk under the water, he felt himself leaving his body and 'tumbled' into an "elsewhere." He says, "I never mentioned this experience to anyone – not to my partner or my family. I was too afraid they would take me for a fanatic or that they would "spoil" this memory, which I find, with many years of hindsight, marvellous. I've never read any other testimonies in the press and there are quite a few as its less taboo than it was before, nor any books on the subject. I know there are works which are fairly well-known but I did not want to. I'm afraid it will "parasitize" my memory or worse, that it will modify it. I didn't know how to swim well at the time, and I remember falling and letting myself sink. I remember the water temperature also grabbing me when I fell. I couldn't breathe I was so scared. I began to

Near-Death Experiences

hyperventilate and drink the water. Then, I remember having this horrible sensation of falling even deeper. Then suddenly there was this black veil, and at the side, a kind of tunnel. A blue cloud tunnel. This tunnel attracts me because there is a sort of energy at the end. I am no longer aware of my body, the swimming pool, nor the temperature of the water. Suddenly, I have the feeling of warmth, like when the sun caresses your skin; but it's almost incomparable, indescribable – the heat on the skin when I'm no longer aware of my body. It's like an energy. That's it – I'm just energy. I am no longer anything else. I feel something so powerful, that feeling of unconditional love washing over me. A kind of bliss, like total ecstasy. And it never leaves me. It's so intense, this feeling of unity, of serenity, of peace. It's so strong. And then I saw images from my parents, my friends, my loved ones. In my mind, these images scroll through the tunnel. And I apologise to them for not saying goodbye. We don't talk to each other because there's no need to talk here. We understand each other. I don't know how to explain it. There are no more bodies, words, but we communicate with each other. It's so beautiful and peaceful to say goodbye. I see my grandparents. I've only seen them in photos, they died before I was born. All come to meet me. They pass in front of me. They "talk" to me, always without words. And here they make me understand that this is not the time for me to leave. That what I feel here, in this tunnel,

Near-Death Experiences

I have the right to feel but that I can't stay – it's not my place yet. I am not afraid, not for a second. Everything seems absolutely normal to me. To be sad here in this tunnel, it doesn't make sense. I still have this energy – the unconditional love that surrounds me, encompasses me, with all my being. Everything is beautiful, good, pure and positive. But suddenly I'm on the edge of the pool again, with my classmates and my teacher who surround me. I feel my body and the feel of the tiles against my skin. It's a little brutal, the sound of the swimming pool. I'm cold. But I don't say anything about what I experienced. For me, it's obvious I shouldn't tell anyone, not even my parents."

"It's an experience that has followed me all my life. I'm not looking to re-feel that feeling of unconditional love again – it's not possible here. I'm not afraid of death and above all, death is not synonymous with sadness as 99% of people. In fact, I'm super confident about death – yes, it's weird to say that I'm not afraid nor sad..."

Chapter Three: Dr. Pertierra

Dr. Miguel Angel Pertierra had a near-death experience. He was an otolaryngologist at Carlos Haya Hospital in Malaga, Spain when he was involved in a serious traffic accident, and he was admitted to the critical care unit at the hospital where he worked. He told Spanish newspapers, "A car skipped the median and hit me when I was on my motorbike." He sustained severe injuries to his abdomen, and as tests were carried out, he lost consciousness. He says, "At that moment, I saw myself out of my body and watching what was happening from the roof. I saw my partner, also a doctor, enter the intensive care unit and they forced her to leave. I didn't see a tunnel with a white light, as other people report, but I did see many lights and a bluish haze. I felt an enormous sensation of well-being, peace and tranquillity. I must have been like this for 15 minutes, until I suddenly fell on my body. When I recovered, I was touched for months without telling anyone, until I made up my mind and asked my partner if they had indeed taken her out of the unit as I had

Near-Death Experiences

seen. She said, 'Yes.' The truth is something happened to me which I have no medical explanation, which has radically changed my life - to the point that I am no longer afraid of death." He adds, "There are cases in which the facts reported by patients cannot be explained. I have studied cases similar to mine, such as that of a woman on whom I operated urgently and who described to me in great details the medical forceps we'd used, which are very specific to my speciality and which anyone not a surgeon would not know about, and despite entering the hospital in a coma. In other cases, people have reported conversations held 50 metres away, and even events that occurred simultaneously at their home, several kilometres away."

Dr. Maris Isabel Heraso, an anaesthesiologist and head of the pain unit at the San Francisco de Asis Hospital in Madrid, also had a near-death experience. At the time, she was suffering from peritonitis and septicaemia and was gravely ill. She says, "The vehicle dies, which is our body; but the passenger leaves it moments before the vital functions cease. Death for us, who are the passengers, does not exist; we have gone before it. There are people who call it a soul or spirit, or energy, any definition works for me. I didn't think like that before it happened to me. I was very scientific, but now I am spiritual. It took me a year to assimilate it and I don't remember everything that happened to me. I know, with the

Near-Death Experiences

knowledge I have, that I was on the other side and that I decided to return to the things I had not done until then. A near-death experience is a great hammer blow to change your life completely. Mine has done a 180 degree. When you return, you are no longer the same, you are not the same person, you have a completely different vision of the world, you are no longer interested in power or money but in less material things. The experiences reported by other people who have gone through an NDE are not hallucinations, they are real, but people tend to misinterpret these events that we cannot explain..."

Near-Death Experiences

Chapter Four: Claudius

Claudius tells Triesteprima magazine in Italy about his near-death experience that happened in 2006. He says, "Luckily, my wife is a good witness, as I immediately told her as soon as I woke up. I had always been sceptical about the afterlife and the stories of out of body experiences that a vast literature narrates. But since I was in a coma for 6 days in 2006 due to a pulmonary embolism my opinion has changed a lot. I could say that paradise exists – that I have visited it. On a January afternoon in 2006 it was very cold snow. In the room of the Cattarina hospital my body began to sweat. My wife, seeing me in great difficulty, asked me what was happening. I answered with difficulty that I could no longer breath. The doctors were immediately alerted, and they took me to resuscitation, putting me in a coma, attached to the appropriate monitors. As I lay unconscious, I experienced an incredible journey. I travelled a long dark tunnel to a world of blinding light that awaited me, and music that emanated a sweet melody. A garden with many flowers and flocks of luminous Beings that left behind them a trail of light; love Beings. I

Near-Death Experiences

remember being able to hear the beauty of these extraordinary Beings and simultaneously see the joy and perfection of what they were singing about. I heard a voice expressing absolute love, far above that which can be experienced in real life, and spoke to me with sublime messages, telling me that my time had not yet come. I was very sorry to have to leave that place made of infinite ecstasy, a feeling never experienced before. The first thing I told my wife was this extraordinary experience. If anyone had told me this story, I would have been sure that he was subject to illusions and maybe have blamed hallucinations due to the drugs I was taking in the period of the coma. Instead, I am convinced that what happened is real; the hereafter exists..."

Chapter Five: Oscar Berlanga

In 2009, 43-year-old Spanish artist Oscar Berlanga had a serious accident in the Canary Islands where he was living. He was riding his bicycle when he tumbled 30 metres down a ravine and had a near-death experience. He explains what happened, "Every morning I rode my bike. Suddenly, when I was going down a slope a car came, and trying to dodge it, the wheel of the bicycle got caught in a stone and I was catapulted down a thirty-meter ravine. I smashed my head into a rock. The last thing I remember was flying. Then, I saw myself outside my body, floating. I had panoramic vision; I saw the driver of the car calling 911. Tied to my body by a kind of invisible thread as if it were a kite, I made the gesture of looking at my hands and I didn't see them, but I felt them. In fact, I also felt the rocks, the sea and the air. Everything. I had a great relief and peace like I have never experienced. Perhaps the best metaphor is: imagine you have spent years living at the bottom of the sea dressed as a diver with a diving suit and a tube. The suit starts to break down and you go up to the surface and suddenly you breathe in a different way, and you can see and feel more things than when you were in that suit. I was not afraid. It was as if I had been in that situation before. An experience beyond the limit of our senses. I was overwhelmed with such joy and curiosity that I wanted to look up at the sky because I was face down, observing my body."

Looking back at this experience, Oscar says, "Over the years and thinking about it, I think it was a journey inward and not outward, as we usually identify it. I saw that light at the end (of the tunnel) and it was so intense that I was surprised that it didn't blind me; it was alive and pulsing, like a liquid light that gave off an inexplicable love…"

Near-Death Experiences

Chapter Six: Siri Karlsen

Siri Karlsen was interviewed by Femina Magazine in Denmark about her near-death experience, which occurred after a routine operation. As she was recovering from the operation, she developed severe blood poisoning and a bacterial infection. When she woke up after two days in a coma in the ICU, she was a changed woman. She says, "In my coma, I had some very strong and beautiful experiences in another reality. When I woke up, I thought, 'God, how beautiful that was.' Even though I was in pain, I felt incredibly happy and full of overwhelming power." In fact, this wasn't her first near-death experience. At the age of 4, she'd drowned and 'died.' She recalls, "I saw a light. It felt loving, clean and enveloping. It gave me tremendous joy, and when I've been most unhappy, I've been able to draw strength from that experience from childhood." In her adult near-death experience, she says, "I surrendered to dancing through a globe in a very stimulating rhythm - almost like young people at a techno party." She heard a voice asking her if she would live or die. "To my surprise, I answered, 'Thy will be done, but if I have anything to say, I want to be on Earth.' The paradoxical thing was I wasn't really happy in my life. Living was mostly something I just did." But all that changed when she came back. "I always had an undertone of sadness in me. But for those of us who have had an nde, it's more important how it affects us afterwards - because our worlds have changed profoundly. The experience has had an extreme influence on my life, as every cell in my body is changed. I woke up with a completely new enthusiasm for life. I had been cleansed of the sadness and feeling of being different that had always followed me. Now it didn't hurt anymore. There had been a kind of blur or perhaps rather a distance between me and my real self. Suddenly I understand many of the patterns of my life. I have become the whole package, where there is no longer a distinction between my body and soul... I cannot separate myself from that experience. It was uniquely beautiful. Just the thought of it can bring tears to my eyes, because it touches me really deeply. And my fear of dying has completely disappeared..."

Near-Death Experiences

Chapter Seven: David Milarch

David Milarch had total renal failure which resulted in his near-death experience. Now in his 60's, he says the experience led to a profound change in the way he lived his life. A self-confessed "wild-soul" he was a hard-drinking, hard-living, chain smoking man living his life to the full and spending most of his time with fellow bikers. But he turned his back on all that after his near-death experience and promised himself he would dedicate his life to preserving the world's oldest endangered trees. In fact, he would go on to establish the Archangel Ancient Tree Archive, a not-for-profit charity based in Michigan. He's told his story to many outlets including Michigan's Northern Express. He says, "I was near death. My body was shutting down. I lay in my bed, barely aware with my wife and my mother next to my side. All I felt was sadness and regret. I was an alcoholic and too often an embarrassment. What a waste. I could barely breathe." He had tried to go cold turkey, and now his liver and kidneys were shutting down. He was taken to the E.R.

Near-Death Experiences

where he was given a blood transfusion and then put on dialysis. The doctors told him this would give him a chance to say goodbye to his loved ones. "I was barely alive," he says. He was just 41 years old, and he was taken back home to the family farm to die. Lying there in bed, he says, "Suddenly, I felt a hard pulse in my chest, like a thud. I floated from the bed toward the ceiling. I looked down. My body lay in the bed lifeless. I looked awful; my skin was yellow and grey. Is this it, thought? I felt a touch, gentle yet firm, on my arm. I turned to see a beautiful female in a radiant white gown. 'We know you're scared,' she said. 'But we're here to help.' "Who are you?" 'We're here to help you,' she repeated. On his other side another female appeared, who looked just like the other lady beside him. Were they angels, he wondered? "We left the house and entered a tunnel of light. The walls were a brilliant white, with a pink and blue helix running through it. Then we shot off and I stepped onto a vista and below me was a white sandy beach leading to water. In the distance, he could see a glowing metropolis, lit by a prism of light. "I felt unconditional love all around me, like waves caressing me. My sadness and sense of failure left me. I wanted to stay here forever. Dozens of light Beings, radiant and glowing persons walked towards me on top of the water. They didn't have wings. They wore white gowns, but the light around each of them was golden. In the midst of them was another angel, a towering presence. He

Near-Death Experiences

looked at least ten feet tall. He was leading the others. I heard a booming sound like thunder. It was the lead angel. "You can't stay. You must go back. You have work to do." David didn't want to leave, but before he could argue, he found himself hurtling through a white tunnel with the first two figures. He was lowered back into his body and then they were gone. "Wait, wait," he shouted, springing up in bed. Each day after that, he got a little bit better until he was fully recovered and able to get out of bed. "Every morning and night I saw a small white glow near the ceiling. I lived for those moments, an assurance that God was still with me," he says.

After David's extraordinary experience, he was a changed man. "I have a compassion I'd never had before. I couldn't understand it." A few months later, after day upon day of puzzling over what work he was supposed to do now that he was back in his body, he woke up to a blinding light in the bedroom. He spoke to the light, "Tell me what I need to do." He heard a reply, "Get a pen and pad and go to the living room." He did as instructed and sat in his armchair in the living room waiting, but the voice was gone and gradually he felt himself falling asleep. When he woke with a start sometime later, he looked down at the notepad in his lap to discover that it was filled with writing; page after page of details about how he could save dying trees by cloning and reforesting them. It was definitely his own

Near-Death Experiences

handwriting, yet he had never had any of these thoughts before and no memory of writing any of it. The plan, as he had written it down, was to clone the biggest hardiest trees that had lived for hundreds of years. "There had to be a mistake - I wasn't a scientist. I didn't know the first thing about cloning or the environment." Yet, within twelve months he had collected DNA from a maple tree and learnt how to clone trees. The result was his founding of the Archangel Ancient Tree Archive, and its mission to restore "the lungs of the planet".

Near-Death Experiences

Chapter Eight: Kate Cliff

The Sunday Herald of Australia spoke to 36-year-old Kate Cliff, who was a busy lawyer before her near-death experience in 2011. After her experience, she changed her life dramatically. She's now a meditation instructor. Her near-death experience happened one day when she was at work. Her job as a lawyer meant very long hours, from 7a.m. to 8p.m. and she was often exhausted. She explains what happened that day, "I must have walked onto the pedestrian crossing. I was in the middle of the crossing when a car propelled me into the air and onto the ground. I was no longer in my body, instead I was witnessing everything as if I were a bystander. I saw my body laid out on the road. I was an atheist before, but now I know there's something bigger than us out there - and that has brought me peace. The world is whispering to us, we just need to pay attention to what it's telling us..."

The Herald also spoke to 40-year-old Mia Dyson, who had a near-death experience after her heart stopped one day. She says, "There was no warning of what was about to happen. What has stayed with me is how peaceful I felt. There was no fear, and even though I could hear Karl (her husband), I already felt far away. The terror in his voice didn't impact on the peaceful feeling that had taken over me." As her husband administered CPR, he eventually manged to get Mia back, and she went on to have open heart surgery. "I feel freer to express my love. What happened to me permeated every atom of my being..."

Chapter Nine: Christine Stein

In April 2000, 19-year-old Christine Stein was clinically dead for 23 minutes. She'd been travelling with her mother in the family's station wagon, listening to songs on the radio, when a truck hit them as they sat at a stop sign. The crash caused Christine's main artery to rupture, and she had a brain haemorrhage, along with multiple bone fractures. The fire crew had to cut her out of the vehicle, and she was flown to the hospital by helicopter, where she was rushed into the operating theatre. Her artery was sewn up, but just a few hours later her aorta tore, and she was rushed back into surgery. Afterwards, she was put into a medically induced coma. The surgeons told her mother that if she survived, she would most likely be brain damaged. Two weeks later, Christine woke up, but once again just days afterwards, her aorta ruptured once again. Rushed into surgery once more, this time Christine died on the operating table. Suddenly she became aware that she was out of her body.

Near-Death Experiences

Her story has been told on many websites including psiencequest.net.

She says, "My body is lying on the operating table; the rib cage is open. I float under the blanket and look down on me. I don't feel anything. I'm just surprised. I thought maybe I'm an angel now. I felt so easy, and then there is this light. It is wonderful. Everything was warm, even the ground under my feet. My grandparents came up to me. They call me and hug me. I realised I have to be in heaven. And that's when I felt completely normal." At the same time, she could see her mother and father. "They were sitting in the waiting room of the hospital praying and crying. I wanted to tell them that I'm fine." Then, she heard her grandparents say, 'Tine, you have to say goodbye. Your time has not come yet. You still have a big job ahead of you.' Then, a sensation of tingling filled her body and she found herself back in the operating room. "I heard the surgeons saying, "We have her again." Christine says, "When I said goodbye to my grandparents, I cried. Later, the surgeons confirmed my tears - although it is physically impossible to cry during anaesthia!" Christine also described her grandparents to her mother. She'd never met them when they were alive because they'd died when she was very young....

Near-Death Experiences

Chapter Ten: Dr. Bellg

Critical Care doctor Laurin Bellg has spoken about one of her patient's near-death experiences. The patient, Chester (a pseudonym) is a retired foundry worker aged 74. He had a heart attack and was rushed to Appleton hospital in Wisconsin, where he was transferred to the critical care unit where Dr. Bellg worked. In the critical care unit, Chester had 3 more heart attacks over the next 72 hours. A few weeks later, when Chester came back to the hospital for a follow-up appointment with Dr. Bellg, he told her what had happened to him when he'd been 'dead.' He told her that he had heard a conversation between his wife and daughter who were at the hospital. They weren't in the room with Chester at the time - they were far away in a waiting room. They'd been discussing a tree they could see out of the window of the waiting room. They liked the colour of the leaves on the tree and they had jokingly asked each other if it would be stealing if they took a clipping of the tree home with them. Later, Dr.Bellg confirmed the accuracy of this conversation with Chester's wife and daughter. It was impossible that Chester could have seen this

Near-Death Experiences

tree - he hadn't been anywhere near the waiting room, and he'd been unconscious when he'd been rushed into the emergency room at the hospital. Chester also told the doctor how he had heard his 2-year-old grandson crying and then laughing and talking about a green tractor knocking down a wall that he'd made from some toy blocks. Later, Chester's daughter explained that she'd brought her son the green tractor from the hospital shop to keep him entertained while she and Chester's wife waited for news about Chester. Again, Dr. Bellg verified these details with Chester's daughter, and found them to be completely accurate...

Near-Death Experiences

Chapter Eleven: Dennis Hale

The ship the Danile J. Morrell sank in November 1966 in Lake Huron. There was just one survivor, Dennis Hale. Twenty-nine sailors lost their lives that night. They'd all set out on the trip, but only Hale returned alive after clinging to his life raft for 38 hours. After the traumatic experience, Hale went to talk to his priest, who told him, "Keep this to yourself, they'll all think you're crazy." Hale's job aboard the ship was watchman - to look out for hazards on the lake. On the night the ship went down, the crew had eaten dinner in the galley, then retired to bed in their bunks. There'd been no bad weather reports and all the crew were soundly asleep when a loud bang woke them up; followed by a sudden lurch. Hale rose from his bunk and went to turn on the light, but it wouldn't come on. As he scrambled around in the dark for his clothes, Hale manged to find his life jacket and ran up to the deck. He quickly discovered from his crew mates that the ship's hull had split. Giant waves were now pummelling the ship, and the ship was being broken apart.

Near-Death Experiences

Within moments, the ship had broken in two. Hale and some of the other crew manged to get into a life raft, but as it bobbed about in the icy water, the stern of the ship came straight at them, knocking them out of the raft and into the freezing water. After several futile attempts, Hale managed to grab onto the life raft and desperately clung to it. Three other members of crew managed to join him; but the waves lashed them all night and by morning, the other three were dead. Hale prayed to be saved. The next night, it snowed heavily, and Hale was barely alive by morning. Desperately thirsty, he sucked on a piece of ice until suddenly he heard a booming voice, "Stop eating the ice!" There, standing in front of Hale was a stranger with white hair and bushy eyebrows. Hale thought he had to be hallucinating. Suddenly, he felt himself rising upwards, going up in the clouds. He could see the bodies of his dead crew members lying in the life raft. His own body lay among them, but he felt unafraid, safe. He felt himself come to a halt and he found himself standing in a field full of flowers. A nearby man was beckoning to him. He took hold of Hale's hand and began to tell Hale things that had happened in Hale's life, from his childhood to adulthood. Hale wanted to know where all his dead crew members were, and immediately he found himself on the sunken ship, seeing them all alive. They embraced each other and laughed and joked with each other. One of them told Hale, 'It's not your time yet. You have

Near-Death Experiences

to go back,' and instantly he felt himself being sucked out of the place he was in and back down into the life raft. Instinctively, he reached for a piece of ice again to quench his thirst. The voice boomed again, "Don't eat the ice! You'll lower your body temperature and die." A few hours later, a coast guard helicopter came to Hale's rescue. He had survived for 38 hours adrift on his raft...

Chapter Twelve: Titus Rivas

Dutch heart surgeon Titus Rivas and his anestheologist together experienced an extraordinary case of a patient's near-death experience. The patient had a severe oral infection which travelled to his heart and led to an aneurysm. While the surgeons worked to repair the aneurysm, the patient's blood pressure went dangerously low, and he had to be put on a life support machine. Eventually, with no chance of being able to breathe for himself, the doctors pronounced the patient clinically dead. The patient's body was then prepared to be taken to the morgue. At least 25 minutes had passed since the patient had been declared dead and Dr. Rivas and the anaethseologist had gone off to the break room and eaten a sandwich after a very long effort to save the patient's life. When they returned to the operating theatre, they stood together on the threshold discussing if there was anything else they could have done, as the machines continued to record no heartbeat, when suddenly a heartbeat appeared on one of the

Near-Death Experiences

machines. Rushing to help the patient, the medical team managed to bring him gradually back to life, and eventually he was able to breathe for himself. Remarkably, he had suffered no brain damage. "He talked about the bright light at the end of the tunnel," said Dr. Rivas, "And the thing that astounded me was that he described the operating room and floating around the room. He said, "I saw you and Dr. Cattaneo standing in the doorway with your arms folded, talking. I saw the anaesthesiologist come running back in. And I saw all these post-it notes sitting on this TV screen; any call I got, the nurse would write down who called and the phone number and stick it on the monitor, and then I'd have a string of post-its of phone calls I had to make." Dr. Rivas says, "There's no way he could have described that before the operation. He described the scene, things that there is no way he knew. I mean, he didn't wake up in the operating room and see all this. He was out a day or two while we recovered him in the intensive care unit." Dr. Catteneo confirmed the same. "I don't have a rational explanation to this. I do know that this happened. The patient had close to no physiological life, no heartbeat, no blood pressure, no respiratory function. We had pronounced him dead and told the wife he had died..."

Chapter Thirteen: George de Benneville

French aristocrat George de Benneville was born in London in 1703 and raised in the Royal Court. In his youth he served in the Navy and travelled the world. Then he studied to become a doctor. In his memoirs he wrote about his near-death experience, centuries before these experiences became well-known. 'I felt myself die by degrees. I was separated from my body and saw the people washing it according to custom. I had a great desire to be free of the sight of my body and immediately I was drawn up as in a cloud. I came to a place in a plain so extensive that my sight was not able to reach its limits. It was filled with delightful fruit trees. I found that I had two guardian angels, exceedingly beautiful beyond expression, whose boundless friendship and love seemed to penetrate through all my inward parts. They had wings and resembled angels.' He heard the words, "God shall turn all your griefs to exceeding great gladness." He saw many people; some had transparent bodies, others were of white resembling crystal. 'They were moved by

Near-Death Experiences

boundless, burning love. Their actions and manners were animated with brightness, filed with light as with the rays of the sun; it was the fire of heavenly love.' He could hear them, though they didn't speak. 'They have no need of speaking. The language of eternal love is without words.' Forty-two hours after he had been declared dead, de Benneville awoke in his coffin! He returned to life with a new mission: to become a preacher and to preach "the universal and everlasting gospel of boundless, universal love for the entire human race."

<u>Near-Death Experiences</u>

Chapter Fourteen: Destiny

In 2016, Destiny, an ICU nurse, was working a night shift. She was responsible for emergency response and delivering CPR. She explains that at the time, she'd been experiencing twinges in her chest for the last few months, but she'd brushed it off and carried on with her important job. However, on this particular night, as she walked down one of the hospital corridors alone, she suddenly felt severe pain in her chest. It took her breath away and she found herself struggling to breathe. She was on a break, and so she made her way to the room where nurses went during their rest times, to lay down on the couch. However, before she could reach the couch, she collapsed on the floor. At this point, she was still fully conscious and deeply concerned. Her chest was making what she recognised as the 'death rattle' sound. The next thing she knew, she became aware that she had stopped breathing. "I knew I was dying and that I was the only one in the rest room. I just laid there staring at the floor and grieving for my family." Then, "After some

Near-Death Experiences

time, I was aware of nothing." Fortunately, not long after this, a nurse came into the break room and discovered Destiny lying on the floor. Destiny was in cardiac arrest. An ICU doctor was summoned, and he intubated her while the nurses tried to resuscitate her, then she was rushed to the Intensive Care unit. "That's when I popped out of my body and watched every single CPR and procedure done to me. I was on the ceiling watching. I heard and saw it ALL." She says, "I didn't really feel disturbed to see my body on the bed. I just thought I looked terrible, and no way was I going back into that!" She watched as her co-workers cut off her clothes, and she thought to herself, 'That was my best bra!' Destiny listened as the doctors called out her stats, and she found herself thinking, 'She's not going to make it.' As her blood was drawn and an IV inserted into her body, she watched as her blood splashed onto a doctor. She heard a nurse saying that her pupils were fixed and dilated. Destiny could see that the nurse was correct as she looked on from above. One of the nurses removed Destiny's diamond ring as she thought to herself, 'No way is that coming off my hand unless I'm dead. Over my dead body!' Then she realised, 'I'm dead anyway!' The ring had been a present from her husband. It was at this point that suddenly she saw her two dead sisters, her dead mother, and a lady she didn't recognise. They all looked to be in their mid- 30's, yet they had died when they were much older. Her sisters

Near-Death Experiences

and mother had a great sense of humour when they'd been alive, and they began to laugh about the dress one of the sisters had been buried in. She'd been a size 18 and the dress had been tight. She'd borrowed the dress from a thinner sister. When she died, her son had decided to bury her in it. "She was stuffed in that dress like a sausage. And they were all laughing about it now." Her sister was saying, 'Really, it had to be that dress?'

When Destiny heard the voice of the woman she did not recognise, she realised it was her husband's grandmother, who she had loved dearly when she had been alive but Destiny had not known her when she was younger, only when she met her husband, and his grandmother was by then in her 70's. His grandmother now began wagging her finger at Destiny, telling her that her husband needed her, and she must go back. Destiny didn't want to go back. She knew, being a nurse, that she was probably brain injured by now. The next thing Destiny knew, she was back in her body, and it didn't feel good. "Out of my body was pure peace, no pain, no worries."

Destiny later discovered that, according to her medical records, she'd been dead for 10 minutes, although possibly longer because nobody knew how long she had been alone in the break room. The following day, Destiny was sufficiently recovered to be alert and awake, although she was still on a ventilator. She had total recall of

Near-Death Experiences

what had happened, the exact things her fellow nurses and doctors had said to her while she was "dead." She told the medical team exactly what they had said to her when they were trying to resuscitate her – the exact words. Destiny says that during her near-death experience, everything became so much more vivid. "I could see the whole room without turning my head." The overriding emotion that she felt during the entire experience was one of peace. She describes that she was sent back when she came to a barrier. Her conclusion is "An afterlife definitely exists." As a result of her experience, she says, "I do not fear death. My doctor says I have changed his life. All of my co-workers believe me, because there was no way I could have the knowledge that I did."

When she was discharged from hospital, Destiny spoke to her husband at home. She told him about seeing his dead grandmother. He fetched an old photo album from the 1940's that she had never seen before. In one of the photos, his grandmother was wearing the exact outfit Destiny had described to her husband...

Chapter Fifteen: Ray Kilman

Ray Kinman had a near-death experience at the age of 10. He says, "I went to Catholic School at the time, and I was horsing around with a friend after school on the playground." His friend was showing him a Judo move he'd learnt at his martial arts class. The friend grabbed hold of Ray and flipped him over his shoulder – but the move went wrong, and Ray landed on his head. The pain was excruciating, and Ray staggered away to try to run into the school bathroom, but he passed out before he could reach it. "It felt as if my body had come apart, and my vision went spiralling out of control. Swirling colours that seemed to disappear to a point somewhere...like a funnel. I was really scared because I felt like I was losing control of everything." However, "As soon as I let go of the fear, the pleasant sensations began. I still had a 'body' but it was entirely different. I could see in three dimensions as if I had no body at all. I could see all directions at once. I was greeted by a Being of Light and Love. It seemed to be just a brilliant glow that

Near-Death Experiences

seemed to absorb me inside itself." He continues, "Imagine the most intense feeling of love you've ever had in your life – for your mother, or your dog or whoever, but imagine that infinitely with no end, so powerful and so absorbing, wave after wave of love was washing over you, and I became the light. It was so beautiful. There was some kind of fog or something that obscured any sense of distance, but my pet dog Skippy was there. Skippy had died some years earlier. For all of us who have lost loved ones, a child, I lost my dog; but we absorbed each other. We were so happy to be together again! There was perfect communication between us. Telepathic communication. Then, I found myself standing in front of these golden columns. Like Jack and the Beanstalk, just rising up, and they were stacked in such a way it felt like this was some kind of entrance. I was greeted by a spirit of some sort, a spirit of awareness with a masculine presence. He knew me. I couldn't tell you what he was. He didn't have a body. He could've been an angel. He knew me, he called me by my name and said he wanted to show me some things. Again, he absorbed me, and I absorbed him, we became one, and the love I felt for him was like the love for my dog. All of my questions I had for him, but he answered in an instant. All of creation shimmered and I understood it all. It wasn't like he taught me, I already knew the answers. It was as if I was remembering them. I understood the Universe, how the Multiverse worked. Everything

Near-Death Experiences

made sense. I was told very clearly; your purpose is to love. I don't mean warm and fuzzy love. Love is a far more multidimensional thing than that."

"Everything is made of love, everything. It's an expression of God's love. If you don't like the word God, use another word. The Being said he wanted to introduce me to my creator, face-to-face. God didn't have a face; it wasn't a guy with a beard. God looks like infinite points of light and each point of light was one of us, all of us, every animal, every rock – rocks are also alive, and they are also made out of love – everything is made out of love. Every Being who has ever lived was there in the light. I was still me, but we, all of us collectively together, we were God. Somehow through the connection with all these other points of light I was God. I was still me, but collectively we are God. I will never forget the singing. It was so beautiful. It makes music as we understand it a cheap imitation. It took on another dimension. You could taste it. We were all singing, "I love you, we love you." We were worshipping each other with pure infinite love. It was the most beautiful thing. I know many people have a fear of death. But I have zero fear of death. As a matter of fact, I want to go back – I can't wait. I can tell you one thing. There was no judgement. There was nothing that I had ever done that was not completely forgiven. It was gone. It did not exist. I didn't have to atone for them. God wasn't

Near-Death Experiences

holding me accountable for them. There was total and complete forgiveness. Coming back here, it felt like my spirit was being stuffed into a jar that was far too small and painful to hold it..."

Chapter Sixteen: Dr. Turner

In Newcastle, Australia in February 1982, Dr. Rene Turner finished work and left her optical instrument repair firm with her young son to drive home. As they drove along the highway, they came to a stoplight where a road crossed the highway. Rene slowed down, but her car aquaplaned and hit a power pole. At the time, her son was in the back seat behind her, and the collision threw him forward into her, forcing her head into the steering wheel. At some point afterwards, Rene left her body. "All I remember is I was moving headfirst through what felt like black clouds and feeling that I was being beckoned. My head was a tiny dot of bright light. It grew near as I got closer, and it was as though I became aware that I was dead. I was concerned for my family and upset with myself, but this was just a fleeting thought as I rushed toward the light. I became aware that I must be dead and was concerned for Mum and Dad, as I thought, 'They will soon get over it,' like it was, in passing, just a fleeting thought as I rushed greedily

Near-Death Experiences

forward towards this light. I arrived into an explosion of glorious light, into a room, and I was standing before a man, 6 feet tall with reddish brown shoulder length hair and a short beard and moustache. He wore a simple white robe and light seemed to illuminate from him. I felt as if he had great wisdom. He welcomed me with such love, tranquillity and indescribable peace, but yet no words at all. I had the feeling of; 'If I can stay here at your feet forever and be content,' which struck me as a strange thing to think and to say. I became fascinated by his robe, trying to figure out how the light had been woven into it. He stood beside me and directed me to look left where it was replaying the least complementary moments of my life. I relived those moments and felt not only what I had done but also the hurt I had caused to other people. I was surprised that some of the things I may have worried about, like a chocolate bar as a child, they weren't there, but the casual remarks I had made to other people that had caused upset to them were there. When I became burdened by this guilt, I was directed to other events which had given joy to others, and although I felt unworthy, I remember it seemed to balance in my favour. I received great empathy and love. I was led into a room which became a hole, and coming toward me was my grandfather. He looked younger than I remember but this undoubtably was my grandfather. We hugged and he spoke to me and welcomed me. I forgive him for dying when I was 14 years old. At that moment I hadn't realised I'd been angry at him. Grandad told me Grandma was coming soon and he was looking forward to it. Granddad seemed to have no grasp of time when I pressed for how soon. I asked him why, because she was fit and well and he said she had cancer. I upset my mother by telling her this after I regained consciousness, but it soon came true. My grandfather took me into a large hallway, and we met a large group of people who I recognised, and that man with the brown-red hair and beard who had greeted me when I arrived came and put his hands on my shoulders and he said, 'You must return, you have a task to do. It is time to live according to your beliefs, whatever they may be.' She says, "My memory of this near- death experience is more real to me than what I did yesterday."

As this was all happening, the surgeon at the hospital treating Rene told her parents she had died and that they should be grateful because she would have been a vegetable had she survived. But then, just as he was saying this, a nurse rushed into the office where they were and shouted, "She is alive! She sat up and spoke!" At the time, Rene had been moved to a corridor where nurses were removing the equipment so that she could be transferred to the morgue!

Chapter Seventeen: Kathy Baker

Mother of two and a former nurse, Kathy Baker had a near-death experience during childbirth in 1985. She'd been in labour for 19 hours when it was decided she needed to have a caesarean. As the epidural was inserted into her, it was mistakenly put into a vein. Kathy began struggling to breath and she flatlined for 8 minutes. She had no vital signs during this time. "I began to have trouble breathing. I was reaching for my throat because I was suffocating. Next thing I knew, I popped out of my body and I was hovering out of my body, looking down at my body and they were yelling, "Sew her up – we have no blood pressure, we've lost her." I saw the resuscitation team coming in to resuscitate me, and I saw the silver cords coming out of each person's solar plexus, attached to one another. I looked at my lifeless body on the table and there was a cord coming out of my body, hovering up to where I was on the ceiling. Later, I was told that these silver cords were our connection to each other. As I am hovering above my body, they're all panicking,

Near-Death Experiences

but I was okay. I looked off to my left and there was this beautiful radiant voice who I called God, and he said, 'It's okay, go up the tunnel to the light.' At that moment, I searched up through the tunnel and I passed Beings that gave me such love, and the love was incredible as I passed each one of them. The light was so bright, but it didn't hurt my eyes. It was radiant. There were green pastures with brilliant flowers everywhere. To my left were all these Beings. I was so glad to be free and whole in this light. I saw cats and dogs running free and happy through the fields and it made my heart so warm. I was taken to a house of such a beautiful light, and I felt bathed in this light. I longed to stay there; I couldn't think of ever coming back to this earthly plane. Three Beings appeared to me, and they told me what the meaning of life was, what I was supposed to do, and our future events that would take place on Earth. Then they told me that I had to go back. I didn't want to go back, but they kept saying that I had to go back, and in that moment, I came back to my body. I was no longer of light body and free, and I had wanted to stay there, but I knew I needed to live my life and I knew now I had to live my life in unconditional love…"

Chapter Eighteen: Peggy Abernethy

Peggy Abernethy, who lives in California, had a near-death experience many years ago. At the time, she had a cyst that had burst and caused internal bleeding, and she'd been rushed to the ER. In the ER, she suddenly felt herself sinking into herself, but then floating. Her pain disappeared. Suddenly, she was floating at the top of the hospital room, looking down on her body. 'My body is down there,' she thought to herself, but she wasn't distressed, and she had no desire to go back to her body, because she'd been in so much pain. She began to float higher through the ceiling, out of the hospital building and into the treetops. Soon she saw her deceased grandmother, along with other people she'd known. They were all waving to her. Then she entered a tunnel where she floated through it, coming out to the most incredible, beautiful light. She had no knowledge of near-death experiences – she'd never heard of them before. "It is amazing, all encompassing, loving, peaceful and unconditional light. You really can't express it in human words – it's more an emotion than words. My senses were overwhelmed as I burst into this light. I knew I had come home. I felt this incredible peace. All I kept thinking was I'd come home. I saw my life – I was watching it and remembering all the things I'd done. I watched my childhood, my teenage years, I saw myself getting married. When I saw my husband, I knew I had to go back for him. It was at this point that I heard a voice say to me, 'Not now my daughter.' I was thinking, is this the voice of God? But as I thought about my husband, I found myself going backward, back through the treetops and floating back down through the hospital, back into my body in the bed with a thud. My body felt so cold and confining, like I was bound up. I was back in this world, and I remember looking around, blinking and seeing people hanging over me, checking my vitals, and the first thing I heard was the nurse saying that she couldn't believe I had almost died, and I thought, 'You wouldn't believe it if I told you I did die...'

Near-Death Experiences

Chapter Nineteen: Bryan MIller

In 2014, 41-year-old father of three, truck driver Bryan Miller from Ohio was on a routine delivery when he had a massive heart attack. He was rushed to University Hospitals Ahuja Medical Centre, where doctors desperately tried to revive him, shocking him four times. Afterwards, he was recovering in a hospital bed when his heart suddenly stopped beating for 45 minutes - and it was during this time that he had a near-death experience. An ICU nurse who was in attendance confirmed later to news TV stations, "He had no heart rate, he had no blood pressure, he had no pulse. His brain had no oxygen for forty-five minutes. We shocked him four times and it didn't work." Brian said after his recovery, "The only thing I remember, I started seeing a light and started walking towards the light." Then, he found himself walking along the most beautiful path, lined with exquisite flowers and meeting his mother-in-law, who had died just weeks earlier. "She was so beautiful. She looked so happy. It was like the first day I met her. She grabbed hold

Near-Death Experiences

of me and told me, 'It's not your time. You're not supposed to be here.' Miller later told Fox News, "I went to Church a lot when I was growing up, but after I got married, I didn't hardly go to Church." He said he now considers his mother-in-law to be his guardian angel. Before she passed away, she'd given him a guardian angel figure for his truck which says, 'Don't ever drive faster than your guardian angel can fly.' Brian says, "I kiss it every day when I'm driving my truck." Brian says that during his nde, he also saw her dead husband too, waving at him in the distance and smiling intensely. Brian says he experienced "edenic" bliss in this celestial world. "There is an afterlife and people need to believe in it," he says...

Chapter Twenty: Dave Faler

41-year-old Canadian Dave Faler was employed as a general caretaker on the farm of a widower. He would carry out all maintenance and any odd jobs she required, as well as tending to her horses. He says, "My experience happened on a normal week-night. I came home from work, ate, and sat in front of the TV until bedtime." Then he went to bed, as usual. In his sleep, he had a heart attack. He says to the Out of Body Research Foundation, "My first memory has me looking down and viewing my body from above, sleeping on the bed. I did not sense a thread of connection, just like someone was watching me sleep, and that person was me! I remember being elated at this sense of freedom I felt, and peace that I had never felt before."

Then he felt himself going up higher. "I was worried my body lying on the bed might not survive while I floated outside it, but I noticed how peaceful I appeared." The next thing he remembers is floating outside his apartment, high above the tall trees in his front yard. Everything was so vibrant around him. "I was who I usually was, yet I felt different. The higher I went, everything was vibrating, the colours more beautiful. I began to notice events happening below me. I noticed a couple smooching on a park bench. As I looked at them, I became part of them and sensed their love. I always wondered what a tree sensed. The next thought had me being a tree and feeling what a tree felt. To me, it seemed like I'd lived the life of that tree. Then I saw a blade of grass and wondered what was it like to be a blade of grass, and in that instant, I became a blade of grass. We are all connected. Every emotion I wanted to feel, I felt. Everything I wanted to sense an emotion from, I did. The higher I got, the better the connection. I remember feeling the notion of continuing into space, worried myself whether I could still breathe if I floated into space. I began to fight to get back. As I began to fight, I sensed a thought. It felt like a conversation, without words being spoken. I was told that I can come home if I wish. All my thoughts flooded to my mother, whom I could not leave. In that moment, I was back in my body. It wasn't a gentle thing. I was slammed..."

Chapter Twenty-One: Jane Smith

Jane Smith, a retired teacher from Pennsylvania had a near-death experience while giving birth. She says, "I thought I was the only person in the entire world that ever had this happen to." She'd never heard of near-death experiences before. When she was giving birth, she accidentally overdosed on the general anaesthetic that was given to her. This resulted in her going into cardiac arrest, and the doctors began to immediately try to resuscitate her. "I felt myself rising up out of my body, up through the top of my head, and I was in total blackness." She thought to herself, 'Well, something is off,' and just as quickly as that, she found herself standing in a kind of grey mist. She knew then what had happened. She remembered thinking, 'I know what it is – I've died.' At the same time, she also thought, 'I'm still me, I'm still here.' All she could feel was pure joy. Then everything became a brilliant white light. "I was saying, 'thank you, thank you,' and as I did that, the grey mist lifted. The brilliance was not just white –it was also love, or the carrier of love, and I began to feel so blissful, so exhilarated. It was an incredible feeling of having been loved in a way that I didn't even know could be. Cradled and totally safe." As the light dimmed, she found herself in a meadow of exquisite colours that she had never seen before. "The colours were extraordinary. I knew there wasn't anything that could ever harm me. I knew that I could not fall. I knew that all was well, that everything was wonderful. Suddenly I knew that I was eternal, indestructible – that I had always existed and always would exist. I just knew that there was no end. That there was a perfect plan, and I didn't have to worry about anything. That all the things we don't understand, it's alright, we don't have to." On a ridge in the distance, she could see figures, and she went towards them and communicated with them without speaking. There was no memory of having to walk all the way there. It was like an instant teleportation. The people were all dressed in robes, just very simple robes of wonderful colours, all dressed exactly the same. Three men came to great me. One of them did all the talking. He had a face that was the most extraordinarily spiritual, grace-filled. I did not think to myself, 'Oh this must be Jesus,' I just simply recognised that he was a spiritual authority, and I could trust whatever he said.

We talked by thought, not with our lips. I said to him, 'Everything I have seen here is so perfect,

Near-Death Experiences

what about my sins?' And he said, 'There are no sins. Not the way you think of them on earth. The only thing that matters here is what you think.' Then he said, 'What is in your heart?' And in some incredible way, he enabled me to look deeply into my being, into my very soul, and what I saw there was pure perfect love, and I knew that that is who I was and that is who I am. I am perfect love. I saw my own gentleness, tenderness, harmlessness."

After this, Jane says she simply existed in tremendous joy and ecstasy, and the ecstasy built and built. She felt like she could almost shatter from the pure joy. There was a sea of oneness and life. "The memory of this experience is seared into my very soul. The next thing I knew, there was a tremendous banging in my head. It was loud, it was fast, and it was extremely irritating. It went on for just a few seconds – a loud bang, bang, bang, bang. Then that was over and there was a sort of electronic click in my ear. I will never forget the sound of that click because I remember thinking that it sounded almost like a tape recorder. When the click clicked, that was it, I was back, and I opened my eyes. My doctor was standing over me and he was doing something that was extremely uncomfortable…"

Chapter Twenty-Two: Charmain Edwards

English School teacher Charmain Edwards had a near-death experience in 1980. She had just given birth to twins when she developed an infection that led to blood poisoning. She says, "I've never had any kind of religious or spiritual experience before. That first night, I felt myself drifting up out of my body. There was no fear at all. I drifted away up into the golden light. I knew that wherever I was going had peace and love connected to it. As soon as I got there, I knew this was the real world: this was reality and it had everything I would ever need, and everything I had left behind was all unreal and illusions and empty. In front of me in this wonderful golden light was this beautiful shinning figure made of white light, and it was Jesus. In the beginning my reaction was, 'No, I'm not one of yours!' because I wasn't a Christian; but he said, 'No, but I am one of yours.' I felt this unconditional acceptance and love, no matter what I'd done, who I was, or where I'd been. There was just this incredible love and I could feel

Near-Death Experiences

all these Beings around him; angelic Beings, beaming love. I've never felt love like that in my life. He said to me, in my mind telepathically, 'Because your heart is pure, if you want to you can stay with me; but we're going to ask you to go back because the world needs your love and healing.' Well, I was 29 at the time and a school teacher. I spent most of my spare time having nice holidays and a nice life and I didn't know I had any healing to share. I had no sense of purpose or spiritual calling. Where I was in the light, with him, was where I belonged. This was home - if I went back down there, I was leaving home, so I asked him, 'How can I go back, knowing this is where I belong, here with you?' His heart was a blazing electric blue star, and he broke off a point of the star and said to me to put it into my heart. He said, 'Now you know that I am always with you.' I don't remember actually agreeing but I must have, because the next minute I'm floating over this body that's mine in this hospital bed, knowing that this is not me; this is just the 'house' that I'm living in, and knowing that this free, expanded limitless being that lives in love is me. If I go back into the 'house,' I will be taking on pain and suffering. If I stay up here, I will never suffer again. So, I'm hovering over this body, really not wanting to go back into it; but my babies were only 10 days old and the thought of leaving them without a mother wasn't something I could do, so I got back into my body, and it's as if everything that I'd done up until

Near-Death Experiences

then, my whole life; I had a mortgage, career plans, all of this was utterly meaningless because all I wanted was to be in this love and take everybody to have this experience before they died." She says, "I know that after you've died, as long as you can come to a place of peace with the dying process, you go immediately into the golden light. Those who die in pain or resistance, they have to go to the healing place first - but we are all going to Heaven..."

Chapter Twenty-Three: Martha St Claire

Martha Saint Claire had a near death experience in 1974. She spoke about her experience at a conference at the Sunrise Centre in California. At the time, she had just got divorced and she was on a vacation with friends. They'd just gone out for the last water-ski of the day. She says, "I was a good skier and a good swimmer. Two of my friends were in the boat and one of them was supposed to be watching me. I was flying along but by some freak accident I fell, and the rope twisted behind my left arm and dragged me behind the boat – which wouldn't have been too bad except the watcher was not watching me – they were drinking beer! I continued to be dragged behind the boat. And pretty soon I had what you would call a classic near-death experience. I knew nothing about near death experiences at the time – but I certainly knew I was in a place of danger. My arm was hurting, I was being dragged along, and pretty soon I found my spirit out of my body, and I found myself looking down, seeing myself going behind this

Near-Death Experiences

boat. What happened next was an amazing experience. I found myself being in a dark tunnel. The tunnel felt familiar, comfortable. It was dark and isolated, but I wasn't afraid because I had a feeling I had done this before. As I went through the tunnel, my spirit came out of it, and I was surrounded by the most beautiful colours that you don't see here on Earth. Colours and hues that I can't even really explain but they were gorgeous. I went to this area of flowers then I found us out in the universe. It was full of galaxies and stars, and it was glorious, yet it seemed familiar. It seemed comfortable. It wasn't in the least bit frightening, and it didn't seem unusual. I felt like I was in this heavenly divine place, and I was so happy to be there. I had no concerns about my body or what was going on on Earth. A Being appeared before me. When you're in this heavenly space you know things by thought. You know things by thinking, and so it was natural. He was beautiful. He had big blue eyes, a beard, and he had like a turban around his head. The light that surrounded him seemed like liquid divine love. He was dressed in gold and velvet. I felt like I knew him forever. He looked ancient and young at the same time. He said to me, "Are you ready to come?" It was as simple as that, and in that moment I chose to come to earth. We come to earth to learn, to grow and study, and that on some level this is like some wonderful theatre, and we all play our part, and when our time comes, we all leave. I had a choice to stay or go,

Near-Death Experiences

and my first reaction was, 'No I can't stay,' because I felt like my spirit was not in alignment with my personality. I could see that my soul path was far greater than I'd been living at that point. Heaven was surrounded in the most beautiful light you could ever imagine. This was a place in the realm of God. It was a place beyond male or female. It was like God was all that there is – liquid love and beauty and peace. There are no words to describe this place, and being enveloped in this light changed my whole life. There was an awakening. You remember who you are. You have access to divine knowledge, and you have access to all the mysteries of the universe, and in my case, I saw there is a divine plan for Earth, and God loves us all. There is no final judgement, and when you're in the light, you see who you are completely. You see your flaws and you see your gifts. You judge yourself because everything is reflected back to you. I saw a beautiful golden temple and there were Beings inside who were studying and learning. I could also see that there was a light border, and I would not be able to go past this border and go to my true home because if I did, I would not be able to come back here to earth. I chose to come back because I wanted to be with my young son. I also didn't want all my friends to suffer and have guilt that I had died."

"My main purpose of sharing this with you is to tell you that there is no reason to fear death - the body dies but the spirit goes on. You simply can't

Near-Death Experiences

die, you are a wonderful being of light, a true soul that comes from another place. This is beyond religion, and you have the opportunity to trust your soul and have faith and beauty in yourself. I want you to know that if you've lost a loved one then you can know that they have gone home, and that when they leave their physical body they are no longer in pain. They are free in the light, and you can still connect with them. You can ask them to come to you..."

Chapter Twenty-Four: Steve

Orange County resident Steve had a near death experience in 1995 when he was in his early 20's and working in the retail sector. He says, "I was putting in long hours at work. One Friday I was catching up on my sleep because it was my day off. At around 10 a.m. my brother came knocking on my bedroom door. He wanted a cigarette but I told him to come back in a couple of hours when I would be up." Steve explains that his brother was schizophrenic and had always been a bit unpredictable, although when he was on his medication it was always safer. However, his brother had decided that he didn't need his medication anymore and had stopped taking his tablets. Just a few minutes later, he came back into Steve's bedroom with a knife. It was a kitchen knife and as Steve wrestled with his brother, the knife went into his chest. Steve's screams brought his mother into the bedroom, while his sister called 911. "On the way to the hospital in the ambulance, the driver was asking the paramedics, "Is he still with us?" Steven was rushed into the ER, where surgeons immediately began operating on him, trying to save his life. "As I lay in the trauma surgery, I could see doctors all around me putting tubes in me. I was struggling to stay conscious, fighting it, because I knew if I lost consciousness I would die, but it got harder and harder and I did lose consciousness, and that's when I died. I became aware that I was aware. I was in a dark place. I didn't know where I was. I knew who I was, but parts of me felt different. It was like parts of me were missing. The darkness was surrounding me, but I got a sense from it that it was holding me, cradling me like a mother with a child. The darkness knew my faults, but I realised it still loved me unconditionally, and at that point I just felt pure joy and bliss. I felt as though I was connected to everything, I loved everything so much, and it just loved me back. I never really realised at that point that I was dead; I just felt like I was home, I felt this is where I belong. When I was in the darkness, I was looking for something else. I just knew there should be something else, that this can't be all there is, and I kept stretching out, but I felt nothing."

"The darkness that I was in was so expansive that it went out to eternity. It was boundless, but suddenly I realised the light was there. When the light came into view it was glorious. The light was almost shouting out, 'Here I am, here I am.' All of the feelings of love was still there, I felt

Near-Death Experiences

embraced, I still felt held, but I was also feeling the potency of the light. I'm not sure how much time past, it could've been 1 million years or a nanosecond. The next thing I remember is being shoved back into my body. It felt like I was being pushed through a screen door without the screen door opening, or like I was being shoved through a sieve, and on the other side I was being pushed into a jar. I felt so compressed compared to the infinity I had been in. My first thought as I came round was that I was not supposed to be there, that I had died, and I felt hurt that I had got kicked out. I was aware my anger stemmed from having to leave the place I had just come from where everything was so loving and accepting, back into a broken body that was in pain. I wasn't given a choice, just shoved back into this body in this world when I would have much rather stayed on the other side. So, I was back in my body and I later found out that I had lost more blood than the human body can hold. They brought me back by squeezing and massaging my heart with their bare hands. That unconditional love left an imprint on me, I'm more of an extrovert now. I love everybody after my experience. It's almost hardwired into me now. This is more like a dream, like I'm walking around in a dream in this life. It's almost a phantom in comparison to the reality of where I'd gone..."

Chapter Twenty-Five: Robert Leo

Robert Leo had a near death experience when he was driving back home to his parents' house. He describes how after leaving college he was working in a great job in technology in a research centre. That day, it was snowing and there were blocks of ice on the road. As he turned into a small side-road, a child suddenly ran out in front of him. Robert hit the brakes, but there was another car coming down the road in the opposite direction that didn't notice the child. The child hesitated between both cars as if deciding which way to go. Robert stopped his car, but the other car was coming right at Robert, and it was going to hit him head-on. "I felt like I was going to die. There was nothing I could do about my car with the child unable to decide which way to go and it seemed to take forever for me to get hit. It was like an absence of time. When his car struck my car, I went backwards in my car like in slow motion and at the same time I was looking down at my body doing this. I remember saying, 'I've got a great life ahead of me, I've got a great job,

Near-Death Experiences

I'm so young to die. I want to do great things, please give me another chance.' Then I saw my life pass in front of me. I've been raised Catholic. I saw my confirmation. I saw the many good things that happened to me in my life, and then I was back in my car in a lot of pain. Before the accident I'd always gone to Church. After the accident, I stopped going. I felt that I was very spiritual and that I didn't need to go to Church anymore, but I knew God was hidden within me and that I didn't need a middleman to talk to God..."

In 2007, Robert had another near-death experience. He discovered that he was internally bleeding and took himself to hospital where he was given a pint of blood. However, a few days later, he needed more blood again, two pints this time. The doctors weren't sure that he was going to make it. Robert found himself lying in bed praying, "God, the universe, whatever's out there I'm calling on you for your help now!" Then, the next thing he knew, he was moving. "I was lying on my bed, and I and my bed we're going high up in the air. It was like we were going so high that the breeze was rushing past me and yet I could see the room."

Robert's experiences profoundly changed his beliefs. He stopped going to Church and began to study mediumship at his local spiritualist Church, because he found that after his near-death experiences he could communicate with people

Near-Death Experiences

on the other side. He wanted to learn more about this so that he could help others. He no longer focused on his career goals and became less materialistic. He wanted to help people to know about life-after death...

Near-Death Experiences

Chapter Twenty-Six: Jim Anderson

Jim Anderson had a massive heart attack. He'd been working 12 hours a day as a supervisor at a waste management plant. When his heart attack happened, he'd been resting in his bedroom at home when all of a sudden, he felt a flushing pain in his chest which spread down his arms and into his neck. His daughter was home and he called out to her for help to get him to the hospital. He told her he didn't think he was going to make it. When he got to the hospital, a balloon catheter was placed inside his chest and the medical team managed to stabilise him. They placed him on a heart transplant list. However, just two days later he flatlined. "I could see everyone rushing into my room, I could hear the alarms going off. It's like I'd gone underwater. My hearing was fading away. That's when I began to pray, asking for my family to be taken care of. I knew I was dying. Next thing I knew, off in the distance I see the most beautiful pure perfect light. As I started going towards the light, it was perfect. I could see the outer edge of it began to spiral and I couldn't

Near-Death Experiences

figure out what it was, but as I got closer, I could see it was the words of prayers. The words broke off, going into the light, and I followed into the light, and the next thing I felt was being embraced, being safe and secure. It was wonderful. It felt like total love. Then the next thing I knew I was back where my body was, looking down at it. I can see everyone working on me and I could hear what they said. There were two nurses outside the room looking in. One of them said to the other, "Why are they working so hard on him? If they bring him back, he's going to be a vegetable."

Later on, I told her what she said. She just about passed out. I thought to myself, where is my wife? Then I was instantly in the room where she was. She was praying. When I saw her face, I saw every aspect of our life together, all the emotions with shared. I just couldn't leave her. I cried out to God, please let me go back and be back and be with our children." The doctors administered so many shocks to Robert that eventually he came back with burns on his chest. "I came back to a world of pain. My hearing came back, the doctors saying they couldn't believe it." Robert was still critical, and they placed him in the intensive care unit where he flatlined again several times. Each time, he says he went to heaven again. He met Jesus each time, and each time, Jesus asked him if he wanted to go back...

Near-Death Experiences

Chapter Twenty-Seven: Dr.Martin

Dr. Rebecca Martin was only 39 years old when she had a heart attack. She says, "I knew I was going to die because just a few days before I'd had a minor heart attack and fallen out of my body. When this near-death event occurred, I felt myself losing breath and my heartbeat stopping. I began to move very fast through space. It was like moving out to warp speed." Dr. Martin says she saw the brightest of lights and went towards it. She felt the sensation of going home. "The light opened up into the shape of a person so radiant, and I just gazed right into this perfect love and peace and joy and bliss. It was amazing. The next thing I knew, I was sitting at a conference table, and I could sense that there were people touching my arms. I could see their hands. They were all ages and genders and nationalities, but they all seemed like people you knew. To the left down the table was a man who was dressed like my childhood idea of God. He had white hair, a white beard, and a long white robe tied at the waist. He sent me a message telepathically. It was rather stern I think because I had a stern idea of God at the time. He said to me, 'What do you want?' I gave him the answer that I wanted to know the truth. I'd been struggling for a while in my life with the idea of how there could be a loving God with so much hell on earth.

The next thing I knew this radiant Being appeared at the other end of the table and she was made of blue green flames. She spoke aloud. 'All you need to believe in is love.' This answered all my questions. I felt clear about everything. I answered, 'Then let that be my work,' and I found myself hovering above my body where I died. I went crashing down into my body and my heart started beating again and I was breathing again. I had been out of my body for 14 minutes." As a result of her experience, Dr. Martin went to India to spend time with spiritual teachers, and it was during this visit that she understood that what she had to do was stop judgement, stop judging everything and everyone and herself, and that, she says, is what she's been working on ever since. It's her way of staying peaceful. She's changed in other ways too; "I have more of an extended perception. I can see people's auras. I can talk to people on the other side. I think that radiant Being I first came into contact with, that light of radiance, was me, my own self. My own divine nature. I think that veil between our

Near-Death Experiences

humanness and that divine nature is stunning."
She now runs pilgrimages to sacred sites...

Chapter Twenty-Eight: Emma Offers

Emma Offers, a German nurse, had a near-death experience after the birth of her third child. It had been an uncomplicated birth, but afterwards she experienced bleeding and it was coming from an artery. Panic set in. "I started thinking what would happen if I wasn't around, who would raise my three children? I wanted to raise them myself. They put me into a medically induced coma. Darkness came as if day had suddenly turned into night, but in this night, I could see a light. I headed towards the light. It felt like I was flying towards it. It was enjoyable. At the boundary of the light, I met my grandfather, who had died. He was dressed completely in white and looked younger than I remembered, but the essential thing was not seeing him but feeling him. It was a connection of our hearts. We had an exchange, and that exchange was at the level of our hearts. I also knew that there were other people around me. The surroundings were warm, and I felt the love. I felt complete and I felt strong, and I felt safe. My grandfather was there with me. After I

Near-Death Experiences

returned, it was difficult for me. I felt like I didn't want to organise my life here. I wanted to go back to that warmth and that loving, that emotion, I wanted to go back there but I couldn't..."

Chapter Twenty-Nine: Barbara Whitefield

After surgery, Barbara Whitfield suffered severe internal bleeding. Her blood pressure dropped, and her vital signs began to shut down. She was in intense pain and began screaming. "People began running, bringing machinery and tubes. I remember screaming for them to leave me alone. I lost consciousness and the next thing I knew I was out in the hallway. I looked back behind me, and I couldn't see anybody, and I realised I shouldn't be out in the hallway and that if they caught me there, I'd be in big trouble, so I turned around to go back to my room but then I realised something. As I was walking back to my room, I began looking into a speaker – it was a PA speaker, and this was weird because I knew that they were up near the ceiling, but I was looking directly into it, so then I knew something was really strange.

I moved back into my room and then I saw my own body. It didn't bother me. I feel very peaceful and calm and that it was okay; that she

Near-Death Experiences

was down there, and I was up here where I was. I remember laughing because I could see my body had tape around my nose, and it looked funny.

I had no problem with the separation, but then the next thing I knew was that I was in total blackness and I was thinking my eyes weren't working, but then I felt as if hands came around the back of me and pulled me into this warm soft lush love which was my grandmother. She'd been dead for 14 years and when she died, I thought that was it – all over. I never gave any more thought because when people are dead, they are dead, but I had absolutely no doubt at all that this was my grandmother.

I realised then that everything I had ever believed was wrong. The reality was my grandmother and I were together again. All the love we had for each other came alive and I stayed with her for a while. Then I started moving again, and as I looked, I could see energy churning and light was coming out and moving to the end of wherever I was going towards. I wanted to get there. The next thing I knew, it was morning and there were two nurses in my room. I tried to tell them I'd left my room last night, but I couldn't. Then a few days later it happened again. There was a very strong presence, a Being that was an Energy or force, an energy that moved through me but was me. The intensity of this love was so warm. It held me up. I realised I'd been an atheist until

Near-Death Experiences

that moment. I had the first realisation that we are not all separate beings. The universe is benevolent..."

Near-Death Experiences

Chapter Thirty: Chris Markey

Chris Markey was in hospital, totally unresponsive. All his vital signs had shut down. But he was conscious of something. "There was a mountain behind me, with a big winding road, and on that road, there were so many people going up and down, that it looked like a beehive. At the top of the hill was a man. He looked an awful lot like Jesus. He looked to be about 15 feet tall with long hair, a beard and the most piercing and kind eyes. He asked the question, 'What did you do for your fellow man?' Then it's like a life review and any time you're stuck and you don't recall, one of the walls comes alive as the movie of your life and it shows you're doing something for your fellow man. For me it was when I was 10 years old. I didn't know I did something for somebody then, but the world came alive and there I was at the crossing guard at my grammar school, and I took responsibility so seriously, especially with the little ones, and so in this place that I was in, and I call it paradise, I saw on this wall what I have done for my fellow man. And then, bam, I was back in my body, you never saw it coming, like a truck hit me. Coming back was awful. I wouldn't wish it on my worst enemy."

Chris was still being operated on in surgery, and he had a second cardiac arrest. This time he says he was told he was not ready to stay there, he was told he had to do more work here. "I started to hear this chorus of singing. They were singing my mother's name and asking, could they bring her out? My mother had been an amazing homemaker and she had an incredible way of knowing what was going on in my life. I would've been so happy to see her again. The singing was like a Gregorian chant, with the same request, could they bring my mother out. I was wishing so much that would happen, but they were told 'no' by the guy on the mountain. He very clearly said, 'No, not now.' And then I was back in the hospital bed again. I spent seven days recuperating in the hospital and then I was sent home. I think I'll be processing this for the rest of my life. To be loved and loving is what's important to me. To care about my fellow man and to do something for my fellow man is what is important to me now..."

Near-Death Experiences

Chapter Thirty-One: Hamish Miller

Hamish Miller, a furniture maker, was having emergency surgery when he had a near-death experience. He says, "The first thing I was aware of was the surgeon taking off his mask and saying, 'Pity you were too late chaps,' then he left the room. I was concerned because I had all my faculties still! But then I became aware that I wasn't looking at the surgeon from the operating table, but I was looking way above, looking down at him. The team were chatting and tidying up. I had this incredible experience of moving up into a misty area and then becoming aware that I was in a tunnel, and it was totally peaceful and a place of absolute compassion and understanding. There was no coercion to do anything at all, and I became aware that I was in a long tube with rounded ends, and this tunnel started to form around me in this mist. The tube started to move up, gliding through the tunnel and it came to rest just at the end of the tunnel, and I got out. I wasn't in the tube anymore, I was sort of a virtual baby as such, a symbol of innocence and

Near-Death Experiences

completely without fear but very curious about the light. I don't have the language to describe it, but I went into this area of light with floor like alabaster marble and big bright colours. There were Beings here that I was aware of, and they were completely compassionate, loving and incredibly caring, and they said, 'This is the entrance to this level of life. These are concepts, and if you feel that you're able to understand them then you are welcome to come in.' Then they gave me all the experiences of all my lifetimes, to make the decision whether to come in, and I looked at the concepts, and frankly I didn't understand them. So, I said to these Beings, or rather, communicated that I thought I ought to go back. Then I was aware for the first time, of the huge humour of the Universe. There was this sort of chuckle of appreciation, and this voice replied, 'Yes, we think you should!' So, I got back in the tube and went hurtling back down the tunnel.

I went through this all with no care at all, and the next thing I heard was someone shouting my name and asking me if I was there. I wanted to tell them where I'd been and what a wonderful thing it had been. I came back with a completely new set of values – all the important things I'd been doing before just seemed nonsense to me now, and I was also so much better at appreciating what we have here – flowers, colours, it was all fundamentally life-changing. I

Near-Death Experiences

came back completely without fear of anything, because once you're not afraid of death, there's not much else you can be afraid of..."

Chapter Thirty-Two: Diane Sherman

Diane Sherman was having a routine operation to repair one of her knees after damaging it in an accident, when she died on the operating table. She says, "I saw the doctors and nurses working on a person, who was obviously in trouble. I heard them calling her name and it was the same name as mine! I was thinking, 'Well, this is odd, we have the same names.' Then I heard my surname – they were saying my name to this other woman and I was trying to call out to tell them that was my name, not hers. I was shouting out that they had the wrong patient, but they weren't paying any attention to me, although I realised they were busy – they were trying to save this other woman's life. They were working feverishly trying to save her.

The next thing I know I am at the bottom of the bed and I'm looking at her and it's me! I see them working on her/me, but I feel no connection to it at all, and I was floating upwards towards the ceiling. I didn't feel any discomfort or fear about what was happening. It felt very comfortable being up where I was, and then I

Near-Death Experiences

went up into the ceiling and into a tunnel of darkness. I kept looking for a bit of light, and as I was struggling to find a glimmer, then I did see light and I focused on this light as it made me feel safe. The light began to grow and grow until it was everywhere. I moved through the light as it parted, like a cloud wafting and I was floating. I could see two rows of monks standing in front of me, with the ropes and their heads up, and as I floated between them, I could feel unconditional love flowing from them. The one on the end had a fatherly protectiveness. He said 'You cannot stay here. It is not your time. You must go back.' He didn't have a face, he was just energy, but there was nothing frightening about him. I began begging and pleading with him to let me stay, saying I can't go back, I have finally come home, this is what I want in my whole life. But he told me again I had to go back." The moment Diane agreed, she was immediately back in the hospital. "There aren't words that can even try to describe the bliss that you feel there. We all come from this source. It was divine/otherworldly. It's almost like a fantasy. Our language just doesn't cover it. You feel at one with everything. It's like you're connected into the universal wisdom and the universal source of love. It's so satisfying. You're in bliss. I would love it if people knew they are loved unconditionally; that there is no judgement on them, that we are all loved unconditionally..."

Chapter Thirty-Three: Erica McKenzie

Erica McKenzie collapsed unconscious to the floor one day. She'd been taking diet pills – way too many than she should've been, and her breathing had become seriously laboured. She struggled for breath and then passed out. Then, she found herself leaving her body. She was floating upwards, and she could see the paramedics working on her body. As she watched them, she understood that the real her was the one up above watching them. When she decided to let go, she found herself embraced by the most beautiful light and slipping into the tunnel. At the end of the tunnel, she felt like she was delivered into the arms of God. "I kept waiting to be judged. I knew I was a sinner. I knew I'd made so many mistakes, but the amazing thing happened – God didn't judge me. He loves me. I was filled with the most unconditional love from him. God's hand appeared and I was able to see him in physical form. His hand was the size of a truck." God told her, 'I have more gifts for each

Near-Death Experiences

and every one of you and all you have to do is ask. Be prepared to receive these gifts....'

Chapter Thirty-Four: Jessica Haynes

In 1983 at the age of 27, Jessica Haynes died in a car crash. She'd been a passenger in the car when it hit a tree. The driver only sustained minor injuries, but Jessica had terrible injuries. She says, "My whole body was crushed. My jaw was pulled off the right side of my face and my face was crushed in. My feet were shattered and my vertebrae too. I had no feeling from the waist down. The pain was excruciating." She was rushed to the emergency room, but the prognosis was that she would probably never walk again. She lost all hope and she lay in bed in despair. Then one night amid the hopelessness, something happened. She says, "I felt a presence in the hospital room. A loving presence, you might call it an angel. It started in the upper right-hand corner of the room, and it started to come forward. I couldn't see it, but it permeated the room. I had the sense of being in this dimension but being in another dimension of love. As this presence filled the room, it started to comfort me, with telepathy. It was telling me, 'If you want to let

Near-Death Experiences

go, it will be okay.' The presence continued to grow and get more loving, to the point that my heart, myself, my being, felt very safe and comforted. A sense that I would be lifted and alive. I said yes, and instantaneously I was in a different realm. There was no hospital room, no pain, no people, no earth. Just energy, and I was now a point of light, but still very much me, and my first thought was, 'I'm dead,' and I had great joy that the excruciating pain had gone. My life of hopelessness was gone, and instead I was in a realm of perfection. I was aware that now, there was no time. I was aware that there was infinity, but there was no end, and it felt absolutely normal. There was no high, no up, no down, and yes, I felt completely normal.

It wasn't a void, because there were presences all around me – presences of awareness, of knowledge, that I am me, being me, and it felt absolutely normal.

My next thought was, 'Okay, I'm here, now what?' That's when I felt waves of energy coming towards me, from the edges and yet there are no edges. To me, and through me, this energy rolled through me, and when it did, I became the knowledge. On Earth, you learn knowledge, but here you became it. There was no judgement..." Jessica Haynes presented her experience at the IANDS 2010 Conference, and now works as a motivational speaker.

Chapter Thirty-Five: Dr. Ebby

In 1972, 60-year-old Doctor Richard Ebby was a highly regarded gynaecologist when he had a profound near-death experience. At the time, he had gone to clear his aunt's house, following her death. He'd been up in her attic and was coming down, carrying a heavy box with him. At the bottom of the attic stairs, he lent on the landing banister. The banister gave way and he plunged two floors to the ground, where he hit his head on the cement floor. The impact split his skull in two. When the paramedics arrived, they thought he was dead. They rushed him to the emergency room with the expectation that they would be taking him straight to the hospital morgue. Dr. Ebby explains what transpired, "It was 18 hours before I showed any evidence of life. There was no pain, because there is no pain with death." What the medical team didn't know was that Dr Ebby had left his body and found himself in a place full of peace and love. He looked around, trying to work out where he was. He was surrounded by the most beautiful flowers, which

Near-Death Experiences

to him looked like paradise. "There was a feeling of vitality in this place. It was ecstatic, beautiful, loaded with love. I knew I was in Heaven, because it was so fantastically different to anything we know of on Earth." He says he felt the presence of Jesus. He felt no pain, no physical difficulties. He found himself thinking, 'I am dead.' But the voice was not his. It was the voice of Jesus talking to him, mind to mind. Dr. Ebby found that he could think so fast and that his mind was the same mind as Jesus.

If he asked a question in his mind, it seemed Jesus answered it before he had even asked the question. "There is nothing in the physics of Heaven that is similar to the physics of matter here on Earth. Down here we have five senses, but in the spirit body there are so many." Dr. Ebby understood everything Jesus said to him, but he asked Jesus why he would not talk to him in English, to which Jesus replied that all languages on earth were cursed so he would not speak in heaven in cursed language. The doctor felt that he no longer weighed anything, and he had no pain or discomfort anymore. He had no injuries; he had no organs. "My spirit was transparent, like clear glass. When I looked to the side, my spirit body would take on an opacity, but I could see right through it. It had no weight, and none of the senses which register pain, fright or discomfort. It felt like he and Jesus were flying through heaven, and they could go wherever they

Near-Death Experiences

wished without ever having to touch the ground. "Jesus explained to me that because of the new mind, by which everything is instantaneous, if you want to visit someone, all you have to do is to think it and you're there."

Dr. Ebby says he was surrounded by sublime heavenly music, that had no similarity to the music you hear on Earth. It was unlimited vibration. He also heard it differently, as though it was in his mind rather than his ears. Jesus said he created the heavenly music and that it came directly from God. Jesus told him, 'Every answer you're looking for is in the Bible.' Dr. Ebby continues, "Another thing which amazed me was the aroma. This was a perfume so absolutely Heavenly that it had to be made by God, and for God. Later, when I was back and I began reading through the Bible to find the answer, I learnt it was the prayers of saints." Dr. Ebby asked Jesus why he couldn't see his own body anymore, and Jesus replied that this was his eternal body now which would never die.

In time, Dr. Ebby found himself back in the hospital bed, and he was wracked in pain. "It was instant cut off, and later I was to find out the reason. Friends of ours were praying so fervently that I would be restored back to life that God answered their prayers." Shortly after Dr. Ebby's near-death experience, he closed his medical practice in order to set up a full-time ministry, because he felt that this was his calling now. He

Near-Death Experiences

also wrote about his profound transformation in his book 'Caught Up Into Paradise.'

Chapter Thirty-Six: Priscilla McGill

WBIR in Tennessee interviewed Priscilla McGill, who in 2017 had a near-death experience after being rushed to the ER following an accident. She'd headed out one evening in March 2017 to Woodland Market to buy some cigarettes and a soda. After that, she'd paid a visit to some friends, and by 9.45 p.m. she'd decided to head back home. As she crossed the road, she dropped her packet of cigarettes and bent down to pick them up. That's when a car struck her.

She was rushed to the hospital with multiple fractures and internal injuries, and she would go on to spend months recovering in the hospital, during which time she 'coded' and lost consciousness. Her heartbeat stopped seven times. During the periods of being 'dead,' Priscilla had vivid experiences in which she saw people she knew including her dead mother, as well as seeing beautiful fields full of bright flowers and a 'heavenly' motherly figure who told her she could not stay. "I was on a ventilator at the time. I

Near-Death Experiences

couldn't talk, but I wasn't scared. I've had people tell me, 'They had you on plenty of high-powered drugs,' but until you've experienced it, I don't think you can really change them - I feel like I need to tell people: 'Is your heart right?'"

Priscilla believes it's her duty now to bring people closer to

God...

Chapter Thirty-Seven: Daniel Ditchfield

You Magazine spoke to Cornish tradesman and former alcoholic 61-year-old David Ditchfield about his near-death experience in 2006. They explain what led up to the incident; 'The doors of the train slammed shut, trapping David's jacket between them. There was a moment of frustration as he tugged desperately at the material. Then, as the train began to move from the platform, forcing him to jog alongside, David realised with deepening horror that he'd shortly be dragged underneath the train. David believed he was going to die.' He didn't die - but he was rushed to hospital with horrific injuries. At hospital, he remained unconscious, and that's when he had his near-death experience. "All the noise of the room died out and the pain disappeared and there was silence and stillness. I was in another world entirely. In fact, it's the most real thing I've ever experienced. I was in this darkened calm space with all these beautiful orbs of colour flashing and pulsating around me, like landing lights on a runway. The colours were

Near-Death Experiences

more intense than anything I've ever seen." Then there was a comforting presence; a figure David felt he'd known all this life, 'and two others who used their hands to heal his physical and emotional wounds.' He says, "It was like being surrounded by love - it's the only way I can describe it. Somehow I knew I was staring at the source of all creation." Then David felt the sensation of being 'dragged back,' by an invisible force. "I didn't want to come back but it happened in an instant, like I'd crashed through some invisible barrier." At the time of the incident, he'd never heard about near-death experiences. David had to have several painful skin grafts during his long recovery, but after his experience, he was completely changed. He got sober and began writing orchestral music - despite never having learnt to play any instruments! "I realised looking back on my life that it was linear, just like living on the surface, but now I know death is not the end, it all feels so much more 3-dimensional. I live far more in the moment and appreciate the small things." David continues, "When I lost my mother 18 months ago, I told her, 'You're going to love where you're going.' It was a huge comfort." Yours Magazine also interviewed Londoner 36-year-old Zoe Chapman, who had a near-death experience when complications developed after giving birth to her son, Mayson. She says, "I just saw this tunnel with a bright light at the end. It was dark and calm, and I thought, 'I must be

Near-Death Experiences

dead.' There was no connection to anything physical, as if I was leaving myself behind. I knew I could go toward the light if I wanted to, but I didn't. Then I heard Mayson cry. It was like a shot of adrenaline, and it brought me back." Before her nde Zoe says she had suffered with mental health issues and had attempted suicide... but now, she is full of joy...

Chapter Thirty-Eight: Andrea Von Wilomonsky

German nurse Andrea Von Wilomonsky published the book, 'Segelfalter' in 2012, in which she describes the case of a near-death experience that happened in 1980 when she was working as an intensive care nurse. She describes how a female was admitted to the Intensive Care Unit after suffering a heart attack and required resuscitation, even though she appeared to be clinically dead already. The atmosphere was frantic as Andrea and the team crowded around her and battled to revive the lady. Fortunately, they managed to stabilize her. Shortly afterwards, Andrea left to go on vacation. When she returned, she saw the patient again, who asked her, "What happened to your pretty hair clip?" Andrea explains that when the patient was being resuscitated, it was frantic. "It was the most chaotic resuscitation I've ever witnessed...people kept stepping on each other's toes," and during this, Andrea's hair clip, which was rose-shaped and had been made by her husband using plywood, fell from her hair to the floor. Someone stepped on it and it broke, although Andrea didn't realize this until after the patient had been revived. Andrea says it would have been impossible for the patient to have seen this happen at the time - because her eyes had remained closed, and she'd had no heartbeat. She'd been clinically dead. The patient then went on to tell Andrea about how she had watched from a position near the ceiling as her body was being resuscitated. She described seeing a male clinician step on the pretty hair clip and a glass bottle being knocked over and falling to the floor, where it smashed into pieces. Andrea confirmed this too had happened....

Near-Death Experiences

Chapter Thirty-Nine: Rune Fagerheim

Danish newspaper Bt.dk interviewed 51-year old Rune Fagerheim, who was dead for 18 minutes before he came back to life. The incident happened when Rune walked onto the football pitch for a game of football with a group of fathers who would meet every Sunday for fun. 'He knows what he saw. He can't explain it, but it was as real to him as the fact that he is now sitting in his house in Roskilde with his wife, and the man who saved his life,' says the newspaper. 'Rune had a strange experience. A scene unfolded in a reality without time and logic.' It all began during a break in the game when Rune began to feel unwell. Rune said he wanted to rest a bit as the game commenced again, so he took hold of the goalkeeping gloves and took position in goal. That's the last thing he remembers until suddenly he was lying on the grass. He had no pulse, he wasn't breathing. He began to turn blue. His teammates slapped his face, trying to revive him but it was no use. They called for an ambulance and began to give him CPR while they waited for it to arrive. 'Twice they thought Rune came back to life, but it was the rush of air that they had breathed into him that had come out again.' As this was happening, the ambulance appeared. Twelve minutes had passed and Rune was still unresponsive. The paramedics used a defibrillator as Rune heard a voice saying, "I'm afraid we'll lose him." That was the last thing Rune remembered. 'He heard clear as crystal, and as he remembers it, the words didn't even bother him.' Rune says, "I was completely gone. I didn't even think, 'We're going to change that.' I can remember it so clearly. It was almost just like getting a status report, 'That's the way it is'." Rune could hear every word the paramedics were saying, and he found himself thinking, 'There's no reason for him to tell me that - because i already know very well! I didn't feel bad about it.' Rune looked around. It was dark. He was in a very big black hole where he didn't want to be. He got the feeling of being small and alone. "I wasn't scared, but it was uncomfortable. I sensed I had to fight my way out of there." In front of him was a door on a wall. It was a huge metal door that was bolted shut. 'Finally, he gets the door open. He sees the light seep gradually through the doorway into the darkness.' According to the paramedics, Rune had been lying dead on the grass for 18 minutes when the 4th shock of the defibrillator finally brought him back to life. But, as the paramedics were putting him onto a stretcher, he 'died' again. Once more,

Near-Death Experiences

the paramedics brought him back to life and he was taken to hospital. The next thing Rune remembers is hearing his wife's voice. At the hospital he had a balloon dilation of his heart. A month later, he had a heart bypass.

When Rune was 'dead,' he says, "I wasn't lying there focussing on 'God, I'm dead.' I am not afraid of death itself. It didn't hurt. But it hurt like hell to come back to life." The Danish newspaper also interviewed Rene Jorgensen, a researcher of NDE's who says, "When Rune talks about a dark hole with a door, I think it is the same as what others have referred to as a waiting place. There are two dimensions to a near-death experience: the part that takes place in a completely different world. And things that happen here in our world, where people for example see their own body from above during an operation or where Rune hears the ambulance worker say that they are afraid they are about to lose him. One woman experienced that she flew out of the room and onto the roof of the hospital where she saw a red shoe. A nurse subsequently went up to the roof, where a red shoe was actually lying. How could the patient in the bed know?" The newspaper continues, 'Jacob Hansen saw himself lying dead in a bed, surrounded by his loved ones.' Jacob is 42 and lives with his wife and two children in a detached house in the small town of Stensved in Denmark. 'But he was not alone in nothingness. A small man guided him through an experience that convinced him there is life after death.' Jacob says, "How should I explain it so that I am not declared mentally ill, and they suddenly stop outside in a blue wagon with a straight jacket for me?" 'He is not the spiritual type at all. But he has had an experience that is far beyond the norm. He died. He has seen what is on the other side of life, and therefore he is no longer afraid of death.' "I've tried it, and it didn't hurt. It is very quiet and peaceful." He struggles to put it into words; it is indescribable. "To explain what happened when you lose your life - your body dies but you move on to something else. Your thoughts live on in another system. Whether you can use the memories and experiences you've had throughout life for something new, or whether you get a different opportunity to use your intelligence or spiritual life - I don't know. I just know there is something. It won't just be black. It sounds like science-fiction, but I believe that one's thoughts, dreams, and intellect continue in some way." Before his near-death experience, Jacob was an asphalt worker. He worked long hours and wasn't someone who read his bible or engaged in other spiritual practises. His priority was simply to work hard to provide for his family. He smoked heavily and ate whatever he felt like eating. As a result, his cholesterol level was dangerously high. In the summer of 2009, he'd taken his family on a vacation to the Island of Crete, although he can remember none of the holiday until he wakes up 5 weeks later in a hospital bed. One evening in

Near-Death Experiences

Crete, he'd taken his family out to eat at a restaurant. The next morning, he woke up feeling unwell. His wife asked him if it was just a hangover. They'd enjoyed the local Oozo, but Jacob said he didn't think that was the problem. As the morning wore on, he began to get increasingly worse, with a burning sensation in his chest that was spreading, and soon his face had gone a grey colour and his body was shivering violently. A doctor was called, and when he arrived, he quickly discovered that Jacob had a blood clot. The doctor called an ambulance and by the time it was leaving with Jacob in the back of it, Jacob had already had a cardiac arrest. At hospital, he suffered 3 more cardiac arrests; one of them lasting for more than 45 minutes before the medics could get his heartbeat back. For the next month, Jacob lay in an induced coma with a ventilator breathing for him. He developed an infection which spread to other organs, and he suffered several more cardiac arrests. Doctors tried to prepare his wife, telling her he may not make it. But 'behind the lifeless exterior, Jacob had some very lifelike visions. They have etched themselves into his memory - experiences that have made a deep and lasting impression. Jacob sees himself lying in bed in a room. Around the bed there are several figures. There is no face on any of them. It's just grey-white figures. On one side of the bed, he recognises his mother and father. Up under the ceiling in the left- hand corner of the room sits a small grey -white

Near-Death Experiences

shadow-like figure. His body is shaped as if he is sitting on an invisible chair. The man doesn't have a clear face but Jacob senses that he is nice, that he is there to look after him.' Then, Jacob sees that the bed is empty. The figures are still standing around the bed, but he is no longer in it. Instead, he is looking down at the bed from the ceiling. He has joined the little man in the corner of the ceiling, who has come closer to him now. Then the scene changes - the bed is gone, and he is no longer in the hospital room. Instead, he is standing facing a wall with a hole in it. He is standing in bright light, although he can see no source for this light. He can see his deceased grandmother and grandfather now - they're standing on the other side of the hole in the wall. Jacob feels safe. The little man is standing next to him, and Jacob believes the man is still there to look after him. On this side of the wall, he can see his wife and children. "I think I was dead at the time," says Jacob. He feels he knows what he must do next. He enters the hole in the wall, and the little man follows him through. He's left behind his wife and children. Light envelopes him without blinding him. On this side of the wall is a huge figure who doesn't speak to him, but he feels welcomed. He has no fear or anxiety about where he is. "I had the feeling I either had to fight on, or I had to stay there. But then I look through the hole I just came through and my wife and children are still standing outside. I look back and forth between the figures. And then I turn around and go back."

As Jacob finds himself back in the hospital room in bed, he immediately looks up toward the corner of the room to see if the little man is still there, and afterwards, he mentioned the little man several times to his family and doctors. "I can't explain it. This cannot be explained. You just have to recognise there is more between heaven and earth."

When Jacob came out of hospital, he literally changed his life. He left his job and began working with mentally disabled people. He felt he had to give back to people and try to make a difference. "Now I don't care about making money, I'd rather spend time with my family..." Danish NDE researcher Rene Jorgenson told the magazine, "As many as 90% of people change their personality like Jacob after an NDE. They feel more empathetic and sensitive. When they leave the body, the light can be so strong and beautiful that people do not want to come back from there. When people come back from that light that feels like love and warmth, they crave that feeling again. The little man he mentioned is very typical. There is often a guide figure. It can be dead family members, or religious figures, or figures of light..."

Chapter Forty: Scott

Scott was 6 years old in June 1991 when he had a near-death experience as a result of a car accident that happened right in front of his house. On that fateful day, Scott happened to be outside the front of his house with his mother and 9-year-old brother. They'd gone to buy an ice-cream from the visiting ice-cream van that had stopped right outside his house. After Scott's mother handed him his ice-cream, Scott excitedly ran out from behind the ice cream van, failing to notice a passing car. The car struck him instantly, throwing Scott up into the air and sending him somersaulting before landing with a thud on the pavement metres away. When his mother Karen reached him, she couldn't feel a pulse. She was a hospice nurse, and she thought her son looked like he was dead. "He looked like every dead body I've seen, waxy-looking bloodless skin. I didn't know what to do; I'm CPR certified, but he looked so broken I was afraid to touch or move him." Her husband was indoors, and he frantically called 911, then rushed outside to his son and gathered him up into his arms. He kept telling him, "I love you; I love you". When the ambulance arrived,

Near-Death Experiences

Scott was rushed to the ICU in a coma. He had multiple fractures, including his pelvis and skull. He'd been deprived of oxygen for a significant amount of time.

Eight hours later, Scott came out of the coma and immediately told his parents what had happened. He said he could remember being "punched" by the car, then landing on the pavement. He recalled 'seeing his body' as it somersaulted in the air and observing his body as it lay on the pavement. Dr. Richard J. Bonenfant, Ph.D describes Scott's experience in the Journal of Near Death Studies, explaining how Scott then became dismayed that he couldn't make himself heard or seen by his family members. He felt no pain. 'He shouted to his brother several times to come and play with him; but to no avail.' Astonishingly, his brother Graham later said that he did hear Scott's voice call out to him - but the voice was in Graham's head, and he ignored it because he could see Scott's body lying on the pavement, unresponsive. Graham thought he must have imagined it. Scott said he could remember hearing his Dad telling him he loved him, over and over, 'but he could not make his own reply audible to his father, and when he tried to hug his father, his arms simply passed through his father's body.' Scott said he could hear and see everything that was happening around him at the accident scene. Then, he found himself in front of an entrance to a vortex-like tunnel. He

Near-Death Experiences

said it looked like a tornado. He felt drawn to go into it, and shockingly, he says he found himself coming face-to-face with the devil. Scott believed the devil was trying to suck him away from God, and he believes God came and rescued him. The next thing Scott knew, he was in a tunnel traveling toward a light. Inside the tunnel he could see the faces of people he knew. When he came out of the tunnel, he was greeted by his deceased uncle Russell, who had died not long before Scott's accident. Scott said his uncle was wearing a grey suit, although Scott's mother later said his uncle had never worn suits when he was alive but he was buried in a grey suit. Scott's uncle reassured Scott that everything was going to be ok. Then, Scott said the light became brighter although it didn't hurt his eyes. Scott felt safe and secure in this light, and within the light he said he felt the presence of what he described as God. Scott described God as having a yellow aura. There was a smaller light too, and Scott believed this light was an angel. He said he could not determine if it was male or female, but that it looked like a star on a Christmas tree. He said the angel escorted him. He said the angle was protecting him. Later, when Scott drew a picture of the angel, it looked like a sun with a white core. Some-time later, Scott came out of his coma...

Dr. Bonenfant has also written about the case of a 31-year old female he interviewed, who was

Near-Death Experiences

working as a research manager in New York State when she had her near-death experience. It happened in the summer of 1981 when she was swimming in a pool. She liked swimming underwater and could swim a length without coming up for air. On that particular day, she had swum one length underwater and when she reached the deep end, she turned while still underwater and kicked off again to try to swim another length. Unfortunately, in that moment, a drunk man jumped into the pool and collided with her, then decided it would be fun to pull her down to the bottom of the pool with him. She was already low on air, and she urgently struggled to try to free herself from the stranger's grip. As she fought with him, she drifted into unconsciousness and at first, she felt disoriented and confused. Then she realised she felt no fear or distress, nor did she feel any panic that she was drowning. She felt comfortable, she felt fully alert. She felt like she was rising upwards, as if she was traveling on an elevator. Next, a scene from her childhood was played out in front of her. The colours of the scene were so vivid. She said it was a bit like watching TV. Then she watched a scene in which her deceased dog appeared. After this, she became aware that there was a light in the distance. The light grew brighter and bigger as she seemed to move towards it. She felt like she was moving towards the light very fast, through a dark tunnel. The closer she got to the light, the greater the sense of peace and love she felt.

Near-Death Experiences

Inside this light was a beautiful female figure who was holding out her arms toward her, welcoming her. It felt like an angel, and she was wearing a long white dress. The figure radiated motherly love but told her it was not her time yet. Almost instantly, she found herself lying on the side of the swimming pool, after being rescued by some of the other swimmers.

Fast forward to 15 years later, and the woman had another near-death experience. It was August 1996 and her daughter had been invited to a party. At the party, the host's dog bit her daughter on the face. This led to her daughter having several painful operations and skin grafts. One day, she was watching her daughter sleeping in the hospital bed when her daughter had a nightmare. Suddenly, a light appeared in the room and the same motherly figure appeared. The 'angel' communicated telepathically that she must not worry about her daughter, that her daughter was going to be ok...

Near-Death Experiences

Chapter Forty-One: Fraun Cristostomo

Friar Juan Maria Cristostomo spoke to Catholic Newspapers about his near-death experience. It happened when he was 14 years old. He'd just had a skin graft, where some of his own skin had been taken from his back and grafted onto his neck. Complications had set in after the operation and he flatlined in the recovery room. His heart completely stopped. He describes what happened next, "I saw my body when the doctor tried to help me come back to life, from above. At the same time, two wings like an angel took me to this very beautiful place. I saw my Mama, Mary and Jesus Christ. Jesus was sitting on a throne. He had very brilliant white clothes." He continues, "Mary said, with an amazing smile, that it was not my time because I have a mission to complete on earth." When she finished talking to him, Father Juan quickly found himself back in this world. His life had now changed. "Everything changed. Through this beautiful vision I understood that we only stay for a little time in this world... I know paradise exists..."

Near-Death Experiences

Chapter Forty-Two: Ruby Cassimo

In September 2004 in Boca Raton Hospital in Florida, Ruby Graupera Cassimo had delivered a healthy baby via c-section, but shortly afterwards she developed a life-threatening embolism. Her doctors gave up hope of her recovering from it and her family gathered round her bedside, desperately praying for her. The Sun Sentinel newspaper covered her story back then and describes how Dr. Michael Fleischer and others in the medical team urgently administered CPR and intubated her. Ruby's heart had stopped, and her lungs had collapsed. The doctors tried for two hours to revive her, constantly shocking her, but her heart wouldn't start, and she was soon declared clinically dead. The lead doctor told her family that she was on a ventilator but unlikely to survive. He suggested they say their goodbyes now. "Once we say that's it, that's it," said anthologist Dr. Anthony Salvadore. Meanwhile, Dr. Chad Loutfi, a critical care specialist told the newspaper, "The patient was not breathing on her own. There was no pulse, no blood pressure." But, as Ruby's family stood by her bed, suddenly a heartbeat appeared on the monitor, then

Near-Death Experiences

another, and she was back. The following day, Ruby woke from her coma. When she was able to speak, she told her family that her deceased father had spoken to her when she'd been 'dead,' and later she said, "I remember seeing a spiritual Being who I believe was my dad. I remember the light behind him and many other spiritual Beings. I wasn't walking, I was flowing. It was peaceful. There is nothing to be afraid of. At one point, it was like a force - like 'You're not going any further.' That's when I understood I wasn't going to stay there."

When the doctors took Ruby off the ventilator, she told them, "You don't have to be afraid of dying..."

Chapter Forty-Three: Mr. A

In 2011 the BBC spoke to 'Mr. A' about his near-death experience. 'Mr. A' is a 57-year-old social worker living in England, who says he was admitted to Southampton General hospital in the South of England after collapsing suddenly at work. As a nurse was trying to insert a catheter into his groin, he went into cardiac arrest and flatlined. There was no heartbeat. Doctors rushed to bring the defibrillator to try to shock his heart back into working again. Mr A. told the BBC that during this time, he could hear a mechanical voice saying, "Shock the patient, shock the patient." Then Mr. A looked up and suddenly he could see a strange woman in the corner of the room, near the ceiling. She was beckoning him, and so he joined her, leaving his body behind. "I felt that she knew me, I felt I could trust her, and I felt she was there for a reason, but I didn't know what that reason was. Then, the next moment, I was up there, looking down at me, the nurse, and another man who had a bald head." The BBC say that after Mr. A recovered, 'hospital records

Near-Death Experiences

verified the verbal commands and Mr. A's descriptions of the people in the room - people he hadn't seen before he 'died,' and their actions were also accurate. He was describing things that happened during a 3-minute window of time that according to what we know about biology, he should not have had any awareness of...'

Chapter Forty-Four: Annabel Beam

Readers Digest describe the story of Annabel Beam, who was out playing in her back garden one day when she was 8 years old. She'd climbed high up into a tree and was sat on one of the branches. Unfortunately, the branch snapped, and she plummeted nearly 30 feet to the ground and landed in a hollow at the base of the tree, where she lay trapped for 6 hours. She believes she 'died' while she was trapped there. She says, "It was really bright, and I sat on Jesus' lap. He told me, 'When the firefighters get you out, there will be nothing wrong with you.' I asked him if I could stay and he said, 'No, you have plans you need to fulfil on earth that you cannot fulfil in Heaven.' When Abigail was eventually discovered and rescued hours later, there were no injuries to her body, despite her plummeting 30 feet...

Chapter Forty-Five: Jack

In the online magazine Sevendaysvt they describe the story of Jack, a 25-year-old technical writer living in Vermont who was hospitalised with severe pneumonia. During this time, he had several episodes of seizures and respiratory arrest. In the hospital, he was cared for by a primary nurse called Anita. She was there with him every day, until one day she told him she would not be there that coming weekend because she was going away for a couple of days with her friends to celebrate her birthday. While she was gone, Jack had another episode of respiratory failure and he flatlined. After he was revived, he talked about seeing Anita; of meeting her in a beautiful setting. He said Anita told him to go back to where he'd come from and asked him to find her parents and tell them she was sorry to have wrecked the sports car. Then she walked off. The temporary nurse looking after Jack looked shocked when he told her this and hurriedly left the room. Later, Jack discovered that Anita had died during the weekend, after crashing her red MG car that had been given to her by her parents for her birthday...

Chapter Forty-Six: Lynn

Lynn, an administrator of a forum for near-death experiencers has described her own near-death experience at the age of 21. At the time, she'd gone over to a girlfriend's house to celebrate her birthday. Lynn didn't drink that night, and as she left it was raining hard. She slipped as she went out on the porch and fell down a flight of stairs head-first, hitting the ground with her face. She broke nearly all her teeth on impact. "I do not recall what I felt as I went down," she says. "I saw stars going round my head like in the cartoons - not the tunnel like some say they see. I saw a coil coming out of my head, at the top, spiralling upward...I felt I was above my body looking down, looking from above at my motionless body and the blood and shattered teeth." Then, she found herself in a room. "I was talking to someone; a higher being about the path I was on, about what and whom I was and could be in life, all the time looking at my lifeless body. I do not remember saying anything in the sense of conversations - it was more like telepathy."

Near-Death Experiences

Chapter Forty-Seven: Dr. Pertierra

Psi encyclopaedia describes a case of near-death experience witnessed by surgeon Miguel Angel Pertierra Quesada, who is based in Malaga, Spain. It involved a patient who was a middle-aged overweight female suffering with bronchial difficulties. She needed emergency surgery, and it was during this surgery that she went into cardiac arrest and her lungs collapsed. The medical team tried to resuscitate her, and when she returned to life, she told them over and over what had happened. She said she'd seen 'the light' and had suddenly found herself standing behind Dr. Pertierra, looking at her own body lying lifelessly on the hospital bed as the doctors battled to save her. She told the Doctor, "I saw you stick out your arm and cut my neck from the top down with a scalpel. Then you asked for something, I don't remember exactly what you said, it was a number. They opened a little case and gave you a really strange pair of scissors that opened downward in three parts. You stuck the scissors into the hole you made in my neck, and you put a white tube in there. After that, you hooked something up to me, a kind of rubber that electricity runs through. Then something happened. I don't know what. I saw my body and I heard all kinds of noises from the monitors. You were all talking. You poked huge needles into me that were orange." The intricate details she gave the medical team were all completely accurate, yet she had no specialist medical knowledge and had been 'dead' at the time she had seen all of this...

Chapter Forty-Eight: Michaela

In 1994, 17-year-old Michaela from Homer City, Pennsylvania was on a family holiday when they were involved in a serious car crash. As a result, Michaela was flown to hospital by helicopter with a serious brain injury. By the time she reached the hospital, she had fallen into a coma. As Michaela lay in the hospital bed, she suddenly found that she could see all around her in a panoramic view, even though her eyes were closed, and she was in a coma. At one point, she found herself up in the corner of the hospital room, looking down on her body. Then she saw her parents and her two grandmothers sitting together in the hospital canteen. She heard her father say he was going outside to have a cigarette. Then she heard both of her grandmothers say they would join him for a cigarette, even though neither grandmother usually smoked. When Michaela recovered, she told her family what she had heard and they confirmed that this had indeed happened...

Chapter Forty-Nine: Stephan Horenstein

Composer Stephan Horenstein tells Times of Israel about his near-death experience, which although it happened half a century ago, to Stephan it feels just like it was yesterday. "The details are etched in my mind like a precise woodcut," he says. "The euphoric feelings of the event have sustained and accompanied me for the rest of my life." It happened in February 1971 when Stephan was 23 years old. At the time, he was travelling along the highway in a vehicle with two friends in heavy rain after going to a concert at the University of Connecticut. As his friend Stacy drove, Stephan and George found themselves drifting off until they were suddenly woken by the vehicle sharply swerving to pass a long truck. As the vehicle got sucked into the vortex of the truck's vacuum, Stacy lost control of the car. Stephan grabbed onto the steering wheel to try to straighten the car, but the tires were already spinning by this point and in the reduced visibility because of the downpour, they crashed. "I heard the car creak and crumble as it spun out

Near-Death Experiences

of control, driving us to certain death. Instinctively I bowed my head and assumed the foetal position." As they crashed, Stephan says, "I felt no sense of time passing but rather a floating feeling. I felt the pain in my back fade. I felt suspended in time, otherworldly, and euphoric. The experience was sublime. I had entered another world; one I had never known about. The experience was crystal clear and real. I accepted the newfound reality, smiling inwardly, not worried about what seemed my certain death. I secretly hoped that I would never leave the sublime place, as it was so much more idyllic than everyday life. I had found pure bliss." In this otherworld, there was "complete calm, internal joy, comfort. I had encountered a portal, a passageway to the beyond, something that to this day inspires and rejuvenates me…"

Chapter Fifty: Arthur

In October 1988, Arthur was ill with a fever of 106°. He had legionnaires disease, and his fever lasted all week. At some point during this time, he slipped away. He says, "After my return I doubted whether I'd been where I'd been because there were two friends up there. Mike was there in a green Kashmir sports coat, and a childhood friend Betsy. He was smiling. The rest were dead – some great grandparents I'd only seen a picture of and never met."

After his recovery, Arthur went for Thanksgiving dinner at his mother's house. During dinner, his mother turned to him and said, 'I have some sad news – Your friend Betsy died last summer.' Arthur says, "The first of the chills came down my arm. At Christmas I called Mike but was told he couldn't come to the phone because he was dead. I asked, 'How, when?' They replied, 'Last July. He had a heart attack at a golf tournament.' When I'd seen him, he'd been wearing his sports coat and holding a golf putt. I was speechless – validation of where I had been hit like a ton of bricks. I have asked myself 100 times – how did

Near-Death Experiences

Mike and Betty know I had crossed the line in hospital..?"

Chapter Fifty-One: Tommy Laux

Tommy Laux had a near-death experience at the age of 50. He was happily married with two grown-up children and was president of an artisan company that created unique wood furniture. In July 2007, he and his wife were returning from a vacation on his motorbike when a truck came out of nowhere and hit them. Laux's skull was fractured, and his shoulder was broken. His wife Julie was tragically killed on impact. Laux was airlifted in critical condition to St. Mary's Hospital in Colorado, where he remained in a coma for four days. He has spoken to several organisations involved in near-death experiences about what happened to him. He said, "What I do remember is that I was now in another and somewhat higher dimension of consciousness, out of body and seeing and perceiving everything from a completely different perspective; that of the soul. How can I explain that I was shown a glimmer of eternity, a taste of the infinite? What I felt was the sensation of my soul being removed from its physical form and human condition. My

Near-Death Experiences

spirit, or soul was more alive than ever after leaving the limitations of the body that had bound it. Suddenly, I had no limits, I had no fear, I was free to see anyone and be anywhere I wanted. Every time I hear of the immense suffering caused by mourning the loss of a loved one, I realise how lucky I was. There, out of time, I felt like I had finally arrived Home. In the spirit world, we have no Ego, and our true spiritual identity is free to shine. Most of our beliefs are not accurate; the truth is Love. God is love..."

Chapter Fifty-Two: Maria

Maria has had two near-death experiences. She says online, "I remember very well when I told my father at the age of five that I had been in the tunnel, but before having been over my body and having travelled through the hospital rooms, I also told him the dialogue of two doctors outside the room, and that I had been to see a boy at the end of the corridor who was very sick. He got very scared and promised never to tell anyone about it, even when I grew up, or they would have thought me crazy, but he could not explain what happened. What brought me back to my body? I don't know, maybe it wasn't my time, but I remember very well in the tunnel I heard my father's voice screaming and crying. I heard the screams of my desperate father and suddenly I catapulted myself into my body – it was terrible. Suddenly I was back in my bed with terrible pains. I will never forget that light..."

Chapter Fifty-Three: Vincent

Father of three 40-year-old Vincent lives in France. When his marriage fell into difficulty and he lost his job, he tried to commit suicide. He survived the attempt but remained in a coma for 3 days, during which time it was touch and go. While he lay in the coma, he had a near-death experience. He tells his story to the Reunion Islands Newspaper, Zinfos, "I could see myself in the intensive care unit of St Pierre Hospital. It was all white and bright around me. There were people in the room. Then a woman 's voice spoke to me. I only saw her arms. I asked her name, and she told me her name was Marie. She invited me to accompany her. I said, "Ok," and she rose above my body. I still couldn't see her face. She took me in her arms, into the sky. I was not afraid. It's hard to describe what it felt like. The only thing I can say is I didn't want it to end. I saw angels, then archangels. I saw my brother again – who had died at birth, and my grandmother and grandfather who died a few years ago." He also saw a number of other 'dead' people who he recognised. He says he saw the face of Jesus too. "It appeared out of nowhere. He had a serious expression and sad expression. I have a feeling he was going to speak to me when I took the opposite path. I will never forget that moment."

Since coming out of his coma, Vincent has never been without his Bible. He says, "I pray every day." He believes that after seeing Jesus, "He lets us know that he is there, watching over us. We have to keep the faith and keep fighting and praying. Our salvation is in each of us, in prayer, and in Jesus, who gave his life for us. I believe that is the message he wanted me to bring back to everyone..."

Near-Death Experiences

Chapter Fifty-Four: Fabienne

In February 2004, Fabienne suffered a heart attack. She says she fell "into an elsewhere," and came back upset. She told her story to the Journal des Femmes. It happened in 2004 when Fabienne was 28 years old and working as a nuclear engineer. They were having a training day at work, and she was surrounded by work colleagues. "Suddenly, I felt nauseous, and I started to sweat a lot. I wanted to be sick. I didn't understand what was happening to me. My limbs were trembling, my body became stiff, and my eyes rolled back. I lost consciousness and fell on my back against a table." She instantly found herself in "another world." She says she was "enveloped in a beyond" filled with love, benevolence and wisdom. "I felt completely elsewhere. The first thing I thought to myself was, 'I am dead,' and I didn't find that creepy. I felt like I am in another dimension. I know it might sound crazy, but I found myself in a white space, soft, beautiful and luminous with no limit. I'm in an extremely powerful state of love and

Near-Death Experiences

feeling. I feel good. The sensations are nothing like anything I've felt before. In front of me I see silhouettes of men and women who welcome me. They are arranged in an arc. I have this 'coming home' feeling. I know I'm not on earth. This moment of fullness and bliss is reassuring and soothing. Everything is increased tenfold and at the same time I have the impression everything is very concrete, and I appear to be hyper lucid. I feel alive and in an augmented reality, much richer and more powerful than the one we experience on a daily basis. I hear music that envelopes me. It's incredibly beautiful and pure music that I've never heard in my life and unlike any other music. I want to stay here because I feel so good, but this is not what I expected. When I come back to our world, I absolutely understand what happened and why I came back 'to life' in my bodily envelope." When Fabienne was in the 'elsewhere', she says, "I had no concept of time, no unit of time seems to exist in this other world. There is the feeling of eternity. From now on I am not the same. I have information coming to me from this other world. And since then, a multiplicity of coincidences or synchronicities. And it makes me realise I am not the same. I have more and more intuition. It is as if there is a huge field of information all around me and my conscience manages to connect to it. I consider my brain as a TV receiver or radio which captures all frequencies, and which can thus collect other modified states of

Near-Death Experiences

consciousness; a field of information invisible, impalpable and inaccessible with our five usual sense. To illustrate what I've become, I like to say that before I was at the bottom of a funnel with a very small diameter of things and that now, I reach a larger diameter and I am in contact with another reality. For me there is something that exists in addition to what we perceive with our five senses. Before, I had neither religious education nor notions of spirituality. I only believed in the tangible – we live, we died, then it stops there. The near-death experience turned my whole world upside down, my convictions, my beliefs. What I lived (in the near-death experience) seems more real to me than our daily life. I'm afraid of sounding crazy but deep down I know it's all true."

Now for years since her near-death experience, Fabienne has become an energy healing practitioner. She also wrote a book called My brief passage in the other world. She says, "In my opinion, we all need to get out of this materialistic dogma and place the intangible at the heart of our life, because we realise that in the infinitely small, everything is only vibration and energy. In my opinion, reality may not be what we perceive. I think turning to the marvellous and keeping your child's soul is the best way to live..."

Chapter Fifty-five: Stephanie

Italian magazine Ammannato describes the near-death experience of a lady called Stephanie. In 1976, Stephanie was born with a congenital heart defect – a hole in the heart, although it gave her no symptoms and she was not diagnosed until she was 16 years old. At this point, her cardiologist was concerned that she must have an operation – or face irreversible cardiological problems if her heart was left untreated. So, the operation went ahead, much to Stephanie's' reluctance. She'd spent the two months leading up to the operation in dread. "The idea of myself on the operating table with my heart temporarily stopped and my chest cavity devoid of blood confirmed the belief that I had that I was certainly going to die." Fortunately, this did not happen and after the surgery, Stephanie was taken to the ICU to recover. She was hooked up to monitors that recorded her heart and other organs activities, but Stephanie says, "I was no longer in my body, I floated without weight or physicality, high above, precisely under the ceiling

Near-Death Experiences

of that ICU and watched the scene unfolding below me. I say below, I am not referring to only a physical position; I, who was no longer that body that had belonged to me until a few moments before. I found myself in an energetically higher position; a condition that no longer had anything to do with earthly material expression of existence; I existed on a different level and dimension. From this dimension, I observed without being involved in everything that happened and the succession of events. As I floated free, without weight or bodily limitations, I experienced a state of infinite bliss, independent of external factors. I feel myself floating in bliss. I floated free, without a purpose and without direction. I was just floating. I just existed. At the same time, I was experiencing an extremely alive and alert state of mind and knew at a very deep level what was happening on that other plane of existence where that body that had belonged to me was located and intubated in the ICU bed. The thought was lucid and through immediate intuition. It was a different way of thinking than what I had experienced on earth. I recognised that body as mine; but it no longer interested me. I was not that body. I was very happy where I was now, and I was very surprised by the show that was taking place around that body that had belonged to me. I followed this show, but it wasn't the physical eyes that saw what the Doctors were doing; I saw with all my being. It was a state of awareness that completely pervaded my being, and I was previewing everything from this state of awareness. I 'knew' that other surgeons from other departments had come to lend a hand around me. I didn't want to go back there. Where I was, I was floating in a dimension wrapped in a very rarefied soft celestial light; it was filled with a stillness and peace and express unending and unconditional bliss. I was free to 'be.' Everything there was heavenly, I was enveloped in celestially. In that dimension I simply 'was.' And this experience was taking place on another plane; a plane of existence where there was no physicality, there was no time and there was no space. I knew with my whole being that it was a dimension beyond time and space. I didn't want to go back to my body. I didn't understand the agitation of all those doctors around that body that had belonged to me but which I now had no involvement. I remember thinking, 'Why are they getting so excited? What is their problem? I feel so good here.' I knew I didn't want to go back to the body because I didn't want to face everything that awaited me – and nothing could be as perfect and sweet as that condition of absolute boundless bliss in which I was floating. But they brought me back to the body and to earth."

Since her experience, Stephanie says she no longer has any fear of death. "In an instant I knew that the life we live is an illusion. True life is different because we are all the expression of a

Near-Death Experiences

single energy of Love from which we come and to which we are destined to return and to merge again in Unity that our mind makes us believe we have lost. I have had the experience of being One with everything else that lives and vibrates in this Universe. I felt merged with the mountains in front of me, with the lakes; I felt at One with the sea. I felt that between me and the clouds there was no separation. While having my experience, I communicated through thoughts with both humans and animals. I could tell what other people were thinking; what feelings and sensations they were experiencing. I could know who was there behind a closed door. I know that life is eternal and that death as we understand it does not exist because it is only a passage to another plane of existence. That I am here on this earth to open my heart more each day to the experience of unconditional love..."

Chapter Fifty-Six: Nicole Canivenq

Nicole Canivenq, a commercial director, had a near-death experience in May 2003. It happened when she was travelling in her car after a work meeting. Somehow, she lost control of her car, sending it hurtling into a tree. Before firefighters arrived to rescue her, she left her body. She says, "I tried to move and that's when I realized I had no body. It was very weird. I found myself in another space. I was just kind of consciousness, but immediately I acclimatised. It was very joyful." To her surprise, she realized the grass she could see all around her was animated by a consciousness too. "Suddenly, I found myself in a marvellous green meadow. I immediately felt that this grass was alive, endowed with a conscience. I couldn't see myself. I knew that I had left my body, or more precisely, that my soul had left it. That's when Beings of light appeared. I didn't know them. They had a human form but were kind of white light. There were 6 small ones and 6 big ones – like adults and children." They came toward her. "I felt an extraordinary love coming

Near-Death Experiences

from them. There was children's laughter. They were made of human-shaped halos of light, even if I could not see their faces nor their heads or hands or eyes. They were not walking; they were sliding towards me. These Beings of light as I called them laughed a lot. Their joy filled me with happiness and a feeling of deep peace. I was overwhelmed by an indescribably strong wave of love, a love greater than love. I experienced serenity that was unbeknown to me; absolute bliss, ecstasy, with the feeling of having finally returned to my true home, to my true soul family They didn't speak to me; immediately I felt what emanated from them." But then, just as Nicole thought she was about to reach out and touch them, she found herself back in her body in the car wreck. "It was very unpleasant to leave this marvellous reality. A firefighter was holding my hand and told me to open my eyes. I hurt all over. I'd suffered multiple fractures."

Nicole kept what happened to her a secret for many years, until she finally told her mother. Her mother told her not to speak such gibberish! As for Nicole, she was so changed by the experience that she trained to become a shaman. "I had been a commercial director, a careerist and in no way mystical. My accident made me discover another dimension; the beyond. Today I live my life to the full. I no longer have any fear of death." She says that Shamans rub shoulders with the invisible, "in harmony with the Earth and the Cosmos. A universe where opening the heart promotes peace of the soul. I understood that in life, nothing is really serious, not even death, which is only the end of our physical body. The important thing is to live life fully and to love yourself enough to go towards what makes you vibrate and gives you joy and fulfilment because that is what really living is..."

Near-Death Experiences

Chapter Fifty-Seven: Sylvie

Marketing consultant Sylvie spoke to Top Sante Magazine to describe what happened to her during her near-death experience. It happened one ordinary day in May 2003 when she was out in her local town. Suddenly, Sylvie began to feel excruciating pain in her stomach, and it would turn out that her intestines had perforated without any warning signs. She was rushed immediately to the local hospital and given emergency surgery, during which she fell into a coma. Eight days later, she woke up. She says, "I experienced a meeting with two deceased relatives. I didn't have the tunnel of light that is often described. I felt a lot of benevolence, gentleness, but I didn't see any Beings of light either. What I did experience was a meeting with two loved ones who had died a year earlier; a friend who committed suicide and my father. He looked younger than when he left us; he had the same face as at 50 or 60 years of age. Both were seated in front of me like in a living room." They reassured Sylvie, telling her that everything was

Near-Death Experiences

ok. "At the end of our discussion, I said, 'I have to go home. I have things to do!', and then I came back to life! The colours, the sensations, everything was incredible, everything was increased tenfold There were more perceptions than usual." Her experience made her fear of death completely disappear. "I am training in energy healing," she says, "The journey is so joyful…"

Near-Death Experiences

Chapter Fifty-Eight: Valerie

47- year old Valerie had a near-death experience at the age of 41 after a ski accident which led to her having to have a prosthetic knee. She woke up on the operating table, in absolute agony. "The pain was so strong it pulled me out of the anaesthesia. At that precise moment I felt soft, like I was made of cotton wool." She was haemorrhaging. "From there, I was floating. Strangely, the pain had completely disappeared. I felt no fear or anxiety. I felt an indefinable relief and well-being. I saw a light and a person at the start of the tunnel. I don't know if the light came from the person or if it was the tunnel itself illuminated.

The light was dazzling; but it didn't hurt my eyes. What is truly magical is that I did not experience any negative feelings. I knew I was leaving but I was not afraid. I knew that everything would be fine for my children and family. I didn't feel sad at all to leave them. On the contrary, it felt like it was no big deal. It was as if I had been bathed in love, but not the love we know on earth. It's a love so perfect that there are no words to describe it. It touches your heart; but more importantly, your soul. The figure in front of the light was a woman, although I didn't see it fully and don't know its identity. It was a kind of guide. It was a kind of light vibration. She said, 'Now is not your time.' At that very second, I found myself in pain back in my body."

After her experience, Valerie says, "I don't get angry anymore, and I put things into perspective. I only see the good side of people. I really think happiness comes from not judging people, and loving everyone for who they are. I am convinced there is something after death. This experience has strengthened my faith…"

Chapter Fifty-Nine: Sophie

35-year-old Sophie had an accident while riding her horse at the age of 11. A car honked its horn at them, and the horse took fright and galloped off, causing Sophie to tumble, then the horse fell on top of her. A helicopter flew her to hospital, and that's when she left her body. "I fell into a coma and had a near-death experience. I felt myself leaving. I remember the ascent and being out of my body. A feeling of well-being. I didn't see a tunnel, but I had the impression of being in a big hole. I knew I was not alone. There were colours and sounds that are different from what exists in our world. I heard people around me talking to me, and my father was very present."

Sophie remained in a coma for two months. "When I came back into my body, the feeling was weird – it was more cramped, I didn't really understand what was happening to me. Over time, I came to understand that we are all spiritual beings in human bodies..."

Chapter Sixty: Natalie

Natalie, 75, talked about her near-death experience that occurred when she was 26 years old in 1968 during a routine medical procedure shortly after she had given birth. Something went wrong and Natalie suddenly found herself out of her body. "I found myself on the ceiling. It was the greatest emotion of my life. I discovered that I could see in all directions at once. I saw myself on the operating table. I saw the medical staff moving about in all directions. A month later, I met one of the nurses by chance in a store. She confirmed to me that everything I had seen and heard in the operating theatre had indeed happened. She also admitted to me that I had been clinically dead."

While Natalie was "dead" on the operating table, she realized she could see her husband and father-in-law waiting outside the room. "I thought of my husband and father-in-law, who had come to the hospital. Instantly, I found myself next to them in the waiting room. Later, I realised I had walked through the walls. They were fidgeting and pacing. They didn't see me, but I could see

Near-Death Experiences

them. At one point, I put my hand on my stepfather's shoulder and pushed through his body. I found myself in my husband's heart. I knew everything he thought and everything he was as an essence. I was more live than ever, and I was a thousand times more smarter. I saw a small light in the distance that sucked me in". The light grew until it occupied the entire horizon. It was the most beautiful moment of my life. I felt bathed in pure love in this light. I also saw my little brother who died at 7 months. He looked like a young man of 17 or 18 – the age he would have been if he hadn't died. I found myself in his arms. I knew it was him – here was a soul recognition. I also saw 4 Beings I'd never seen on earth but recognised, as though they had known me from the dawn of time. I saw my husband's brother who died from drowning – I'd only known him from a photo. It felt as if the universe was within my reach in the form of a Being known to our hearts. He asked me, 'What did you do for others?' I realised I hadn't done much and told myself that I would try to change that. I knew that when I die, I will not be asked what religion or race I am, but I will be judged by the love I have given...."

Near-Death Experiences

Chapter Sixty-One: Mo Abdelbaki

Mo Abdelbaki has described his near-death experience to Gaia tv. "It's been almost 30 years since, but the memory of it is as vivid as if it occurred yesterday. It's safe to say that nearly dying changed everything about my life and for that I'll be ever grateful. Moments that jolt you to your very core are hard to forget. I suppose that's one of their benefits." His near-death experience occurred when he was suffering from double pneumonia. His doctor had misdiagnosed him and told him to go home. Back home lying in bed, he could barely breathe anymore, and he felt himself giving up. Then suddenly, "That's when my eyes flew open, and I saw the light. I was blinded by this brilliant white light at the foot of my bed. I could make out a silhouette standing next to the light, but I couldn't see it well. When I managed to move out of the direct line of the blinding beam, I was able to see the figure. It was my father, dressed in a double-breasted white suit, smiling at me. The death of my father a few years ago had torn at the very fabric of my worldview,

Near-Death Experiences

and here he was, standing in front of me. The white light had now become a doorway behind which was an escalator that rose to a brilliant background. I found that I could sit up easily and knew all I had to do was jump out of bed and get on the escalator. I asked if I had to go with him and he replied that I could stay if I wanted. I replied that my children needed me. He told me that when the time was right, he would return. There wasn't an ounce of doubt anywhere in my being that this experience was not authentic. I felt loving reassurance. Those of us who've seen it and come back never doubt that it was real. My experience was real. Living in the moment was my true gift from the near-death experience. I know that when my time comes, a friendly face will be there to greet me and guide me. I'll walk into that white light and embrace whatever comes next with excitement and happiness...'

Chapter Sixty-Two: Nadi McCaffrey

74-year-old Nadi McCaffrey from Auvergen in France told her story to Christian website guideposts.org. She explains that she has had a near-death experience three times. The first time it happened was when she was aged 7. Then it happened again when she was 17, and again at when she was 54. On the first occasion, Nadi was staying with her grandparents at their estate in Vichy. The house was situated at the top of a hill and surrounded by fields of wheat. In the summers, Nadi would spend hours out in the fields, gathering up wildflowers to bring back home to give to her grandmother. One summer day, she was busy picking flowers when she suddenly came face to face with a viper snake. The snake launched itself straight at her and bit her on the leg. Her grandmother heard her screams and came running and carried her back to the farmhouse. As Nadi was rushed indoors, she lost consciousness and the emergency services were quickly summoned to the house. She says, "I left my body and watched from

Near-Death Experiences

above as doctors worked to save me. My leg was brownish-grey, swollen. The doctors discussed amputation. That didn't bother me. Wherever I was, it was safe. My body was suddenly uninteresting. I had no desire to return to it." Then Natalie spotted a bright light, "more dazzling than the sun. It grew bigger and materialized into something; a woman, her arms stretched toward me. She said. 'To speak to me is prayer, and to pray is love.' She told me I had to return. 'You have a lot to accomplish,' she said. 'I will always be with you.' Then the figure vanished. Nadi opened her eyes and found herself lying in bed. She'd been in a coma for 10 days. Nadi told her grandmother what had happened, and her grandmother told her to keep it a secret – that nobody would understand.

Nadi felt like a different person after her experience. "When I passed someone on the street, I instinctively knew how they would die, or if they would soon welcome a baby. I knew if people were lying. It was as if my intuitive senses had multiplied overnight." She wanted to go back, to be with the female figure again. At the age of 17, when the desire to be back in that special place became too overwhelming, Nadi took some pills and overdosed. She passed out and woke up to find herself in hospital. "I floated above my body once again. Doctors and nurses rushed around, trying to revive me. I found the scene uninteresting. I was sucked through a tunnel

Near-Death Experiences

toward a brilliant light. At the end of it, I found myself alone. Out of place. As if I weren't supposed to be there. A man spoke. His voice boomed around me; 'You can't stay. You have not even begun to do your work yet. You have to go back.' I wanted to argue but for some reason was incapable of doing so, so I floated above my body once more. It was now covered with a sheet. A nurse sobbed beside it. I hovered over myself and re-entered my body. The pain was excruciating. The nurse drew back the sheet, shocked. I was alive!"

Nadi went on to marry and have a child, and she volunteered at a nursing home. "One morning, I woke up feeling feverish. With no-one to cover my shift, I went in. I sat in a chair at the foot of my favourite patient's bed. I'd planned on reading her a book. All of a sudden, I grew hot. I was sweating profusely. I glanced at my hands - they were glowing. My entire body was shimmering! I felt myself wrenched away from my body. Pictures began to flash before my eyes. Only it wasn't my life that was in review—it was the Earth's. Its past, present and future. I felt the emotions of the world's pain, frustration and anger." A voice snapped her back into her body, and again she was rushed to hospital, where they discovered she had a severe kidney infection. She remained in hospital for several weeks. There was serious scarring on her kidneys – yet when she

Near-Death Experiences

was discharged from hospital they had somehow mysteriously vanished.

A few years later, her son who was serving in the military was killed in Iraq. After this, Nadi became determined to help soldiers suffering from ptsd...

Chapter Sixty-Three: Philip

'Philip S.' was lying in bed one night just about to go to sleep when he reached over to turn off the bedside light. Suddenly, he felt a sharp pain in his chest, then darkness fell over him. He explains what happened next; 'There was a popping feeling from my body and the next thing I knew I was floating above my bed. I could see myself as another person would,' as if he was seeing through someone else's eyes, looking at himself. He could see his body lying on the bed below him, with his eyes closed and his hands clutching his chest. 'I discovered that I could move, and at an expediential speed too. I noticed two figures like me. I sensed that I knew them, but not in this life. They greeted me and asked me how I had taken all of this. I felt peaceful, no feelings of anguish or any sort of pain.' They didn't speak aloud, 'There was no need. It was like telepathy. They were angels, my guardians. The next thing I knew, I was being sucked into a wave or some sort of tunnel of blackness, but it was not frightening. It was peaceful, and very warm. I

Near-Death Experiences

was then released into pure light. I saw not really a figure, as it was just a Being made of light, with no form. I knew the moment I saw him it was Jesus. He took me into his arms, and he told me that I was not supposed to have entered this existence yet. He asked if I had any questions about the world, and I did, thousands of them. I asked and he answered just as quickly as I asked them. I was gaining huge knowledge about the world and everything in it, about man, and its purpose. Then he told me he was to take me to the Father. I entered a new universe filled with an uncountable number of colours. I noticed now I was pure light. I noticed others too, deceased. All were made of light. We entered a huge chamber, another chamber of light. There was a throne, sort of. God was sitting upon it. There was an irrepressible feeling of love, a feeling of overwhelming peace. There were no bad feelings in this entire experience. God asked me, 'How did you serve your fellow man?' I told him that I didn't know. Then my soul filled with my entire past, and almost instantly it was over. God told me it was not my time to leave the human existence.

Apparently, I made the choice to come back. I felt a rush as if traveling super speeds, and then a popping sensation. Then I woke up on a hospital bed, where there was a sheet over me. I lay there, regaining my strength, then I pushed the sheet off and walked out of the room. My mom

Near-Death Experiences

screamed and then fainted, and my father bolted up, as if terrified. I was dead for nearly 4 hours. It felt as if I was in heaven for days and days..."

Chapter Sixty-Four: Maria

Bulgarian lady Maria K experienced a traumatic miscarriage one summer while on vacation in her home country. She was rushed to the nearest hospital by her husband, where she was admitted for an operation that was scheduled in three days-time. For some reason, when the anaesthetist injected her, it felt like she was being injected with acid. Her body immediately felt like it was on fire, and she began to struggle to breathe. Her throat began to close-over. Then her strange experience began; 'It seemed like I was inside a cubist painting... I became a 'triangle' and struggled with the sharp corners of the other triangles. Later, I learned that the doctors hit me at the end to make me wake up - I was slapped in the face many times. My disappointment that I´d left my body to the idiots at the hospital passed and I started to explore my new condition. I realized I wasn´t 'dead'. I had only changed my state of consciousness. I still 'existed!' How is this possible? I have no body, but I´m 'alive'. It was strange not to have a body anymore but still existing as a voice. Strangely, I didn´t have a thought about leaving behind my father or my husband, or my earthly life. Not a trace of regret. Then the light came. I was thrown straight into the middle of the Sun, the warmest, most beautiful, most welcoming light. I´m not sure, but I might have heard psalm singing. It was light and it was Love at the same time. I felt welcomed and loved. I came 'Home'. The intensity is so indescribable in words. Nothing on earth is comparable. Here, I could move as I wanted - where I wanted. And while I was enjoying my new condition of total freedom and total Love, I was pulled down, a force that pulled me back to my body. My eyes opened in a strange way. The first thing I saw was the machinery above my room-mates beds and then their heads and themselves lying there.

Today I´m convinced that God exists. My (deceased) grandfather comes to visit me often and radiates light and energy. He turns up in difficult moments and sometimes warns me...'

Near-Death Experiences

Chapter Sixty-FIve: Dr. Greyson

Dr. Bruce Greyson told WMRA news about an early near-death experience he came across when he was an intern. He was called to see a female patient in the ER who had been brought in after overdosing. When Dr. Greyson arrived, the patient was unconscious in her room, so he was unable to talk to her. He took a stroll down the hall and chatted to a patient in another room. He'd brought some spaghetti for lunch with him that day and as he stood talking to the patient, he ate his spaghetti. Unfortunately, he managed to spill some sauce on his tie, so to cover it up, he quickly buttoned up his doctor's coat. Later on, the female patient who had overdosed was moved to the intensive care unit, where she eventually recovered. At this point, Dr. Greyson, who was training to be a psychiatrist, went to see her again. As he introduced himself, he was shocked to discover that the patient already knew who he was. "I remember you from last night," she told him. Dr. Greyson couldn't understand how that could have been possible – she'd been unconscious when she'd been brought into the hospital. "So, I said, 'I thought you were out cold', and she said, 'I saw you talking to Susan down the hall', and then she told me about the conversation I had about the spaghetti stain on my tie."

Dr. Greyson has since become an eminent researcher into such experiences. He explains that these sorts of situations usually happen when someone is pronounced dead or when they are close to death. He says that for those going through it, it might feel as though their thoughts are faster and clearer than usual. Most people will also have a sense of stopping or slowing down.

Near-Death Experiences

Chapter Sixty-Six: Louis Tucker

In the 1940's, Catholic priest Louis Tucker described his near-death experience when he recorded it in his memoirs. It had happened to him decades earlier in 1909 when he experienced a very severe case of food poisoning, long before near death experiences were written or talked about. When his family saw how sick he was, they summoned a doctor, who came quickly to the house, but not long afterwards, Priest Tucker fell into unconsciousness and the doctor pronounced him to be dead. Tucker later wrote, 'The sensation was not quite like anything earthly; the nearest thing to it is passing through a short tunnel on a train. I emerged into a place where people were being met by friends. It was full of light, and father was waiting for me.' (The priest means his own deceased father.) 'He talked exactly as he had in the last few years of his life and wore the last suit of clothes he had owned. I knew they were familiar to me so that I might feel no strangeness in seeing him. Soon I discovered that we were not talking but thinking. I knew

Near-Death Experiences

dozens of things that we did not mention because he knew them. He thought of a question, in an answer, without speaking; the process was practically instantaneous. What he said was in ideas, not words. I did not want to go back; the idea of self-preservation was quite gone...' But he did find himself back. 'There was a short interval of confusion and hurrying blackness, and I came to, to find myself lying on my bed with the doctor bending over telling me that I was safe and would now live. I told him that I knew some time ago...'

Chapter Sixty-Seven: Cherie

Cherie was rushed to the ER in April 2010 when she found herself struggling to breathe. Within minutes of arriving, she had flatlined, and what followed would be months of traumatic experiences as the medical team struggled to keep her alive and she could be taken off all the machinery. First, her heart stopped and she flatlined, and her organs began to fail. She was transferred to a specialist hospital, where she arrived without a heartbeat. 'I crossed over to the afterworld,' she writes. 'I was aware I had crossed over. I was extremely alert. I remember a heightened level of senses, such as telepathy.' As she became aware of her surroundings, she says, 'I was never alone. I was always surrounded by many Beings. Some in form and others non-form. I always felt their love and protection. I felt safe, light as a feather, with none of the burdens of my normal life. I was able to hear my conversations with other Beings in the spiritual dimension. I saw Beings that had passed over. Everything was telepathic and all-knowing, so I didn't have to

Near-Death Experiences

look and use my eyes the way we normally do. I was able to hear sounds and conversations going on in my physical room, and outside of my room. Colors were so much richer. I remember a series of events that took place in this large house with all white walls. There were Beings of form around me that I was communicating with. This experience did confirm my belief that our soul never dies and that we will not be alone even after our physical bodies cease to exist...

Near-Death Experiences

Chapter Sixty-Eight: Joe Tiralosi

In 2009 in New York City, 57-year-old chauffeur Joe Tiralosi suddenly began sweating profusely and feeling nauseous. He'd just pulled out of a car wash and was heading back home to Brooklyn. It was the middle of the summer in the City and he turned up the air conditioning, thinking he'd soon cool off. However, within the hour, his discomfort hadn't improved, and he didn't even feel capable of driving his car anymore. Not long afterwards, a co-worker found him slumped over at the wheel and had him rushed to the ER. He'd had a cardiac arrest. Within minutes of his arrival at the Presbyterian Hospital, his heart stopped. He flatlined and the doctors urgently began delivering electric shocks to his heart, desperately trying to resuscitate him. Two minutes passed, then five, then ten. He was clinically dead; but still the team persisted, until Joe had been dead for 47 minutes. Then astonishingly, he came back to life.

Before being released from hospital a couple of weeks later, critical-care doctor Sam Parnia,

Near-Death Experiences

director of resuscitation research at the State University of New York at Stony Brook, met with him. Joe told Dr. Parnia that when he'd been "dead," he had an encounter with a luminous Being filled with compassion who gave him the sensation of warmth and love. "We try to explain NDEs as lack of oxygen, hallucinations," Parnia told the New York Post, "but there's no evidence to show its chemical..."

Chapter Sixty-Nine: Chamise

In 1982 Chamise had an accident resulting in her severely haemorrhaging. Suddenly, she says, "It seemed as if I was totally alert, but my body was under extreme sedation. It was as if time stopped, as if everything was in a hologram. I watched everything happening within the surgical arena. I could hear, see everything, as if past present and future were all at once. Everything became so much more vivid. I could see through walls. I read the surgeons mind, and instantly knew he was having an affair with the attending nurse. I could hear thoughts of the people in the room." She was watching everything from above the operating table. "Everything was with greater clarity than if I were doing the surgery myself." She was aware of the light which she describes as "a light clearly of mystical or otherworldly origin. And the light of a holy Being. Always in some kind of hologram. Our personality, including our knowledge and emotions, seem to go with us wherever we are in this life." She felt great peace and comfort.

Near-Death Experiences

After her recovery, Chamise told the physician what had happened, "But he was so scared by what I saw in his future and that I'd seen his affair going on, he cut me off directly. The physician said I was hallucinating. We are spiritual Beings having a mortal experience – the tools of science don't apply. The spiritual realm can't be explained using physical tools to measure spiritual concepts life is eternal. I watched everything that was going on in a completely detached mode. I heard the buzz of saws. I saw through walls. My husband was home chopping wood. I saw the red roses waiting in my patient room from my sister. I could instantly read the minds of those in the surgery room. I observed a Being of light. I was washed with a flood of love and forgiveness for everyone and everything..."

Near-Death Experiences

Chapter Seventy: Gillian

A lady called Gillian gave her story to the near-death research foundation. She explains that in 2013 she had been sick for a week with chest pains and a fever. She was a doctor and was rostered on-call at the hospital where she worked. She hadn't called in sick but had carried on working, despite how ill she felt. On this particular night, after carrying out her rounds she went to the urgent care clinic to get checked out herself and discovered that the x-rays of her chest showed irregular nodules. She was diagnosed as having an aneurysm and as a result, she was urgently flown to a specialist heart unit where she was sedated because her blood pressure was wildly fluctuating. Then, she was taken to the ER for cardiothoracic surgery, where she was intubated. However, an echocardiogram showed that the diagnosis of aneurysm was incorrect, and her surgery was cancelled. On her way to have yet another test, Gillian had her near-death experience. 'I was chatting with my nurse, who was pushing me down a long empty tunnel in a wheelchair. I realized that I was losing my vision. I was losing my hearing. I was about to fall out of

Near-Death Experiences

the wheelchair. That's the last thing I recall.' Her next recollection is of seeing a brilliant white light in a vast endless space. She could see everywhere, in all directions. 'A panoramic 360 degrees.' There was no sensation of Time. 'Time was meaningless. I was with a group of Beings that I felt I had known for a very long time.' It felt like she was with them for days, or weeks. It felt to her like a reunion, and that she was in a place for rest and recuperation. It felt like her experiences on earth were 'downloaded' for her to see. When she communicated with the Beings there, it was by non-verbal means, and it was instantaneous. 'It involved relaying entire occurrences, concepts, and events with associated emotions, not just words and sentences.' Eventually, the Beings told her she must now return to her life back on earth. When the Beings left her, 'They were like brilliant jewels.' Her next recollection is of hovering. Her vision was now back to the way we see things. She could see her own face, looking down on it as an oxygen mask covered her mouth and nose. Then she found herself back inside her own body, lying in the bed again. 'It was a very rapid transition. I could hear again and could hear the medical staff yelling orders. I was hurt all over. At some point, I recall starting to cry and asking them, "Why did you bring me back to this place?" It was so nice there. Everyone was so nice and loved each other. It was so beautiful.' Later, the medical team treating her confirmed that she had

Near-Death Experiences

been clinically dead when this had all happened. 'I felt intense joy and happiness in the disembodied state in the white light. Incredible peace, incredible joy.' It led to a profound change. She says, 'Don't sweat the small stuff, because in the big scheme of things, much of our reality is 'small stuff.' Don't beat yourself (or others) up for mistakes. An afterlife definitely exists. I do not fear death. I was encompassed and embraced by a seemingly very powerful, but loving entity, like I was a beloved child. I recall crying when I woke up because I had lost so many abilities by being 'here'. I have never forgotten that memory of total love and acceptance and being cherished...'

Conclusion

I hope you have enjoyed reading these true stories of near-death experiences. I hope they have given you comfort, reassurance and confidence that we go somewhere really special when we die; that death is not the end and a wonderful paradise filled with our loved ones is waiting for us when we die.

When people from across the world, across the centuries, with no knowledge of each other, have such remarkably similar experiences of being surrounded by unconditional love, of being reunited with their families, and of never wanting to leave that special place, it's almost impossible not to believe in the afterlife and the glorious future that awaits you.

Other Books by Rachel J. Hopkins:

NEAR-DEATH EXPERIENCES: True Stories of going to Heaven

https://www.amazon.com/NEAR-DEATH-EXPERIENCES-Stories-stories-Experiences-ebook/dp/B071LGJX4Y

https://www.amazon.co.uk/NEAR-DEATH-EXPERIENCES-Stories-stories-Experiences-ebook/dp/B071LGJX4Y

Printed in Great Britain
by Amazon